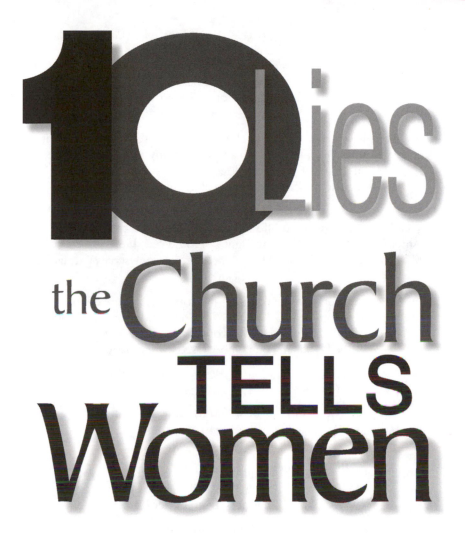

10 Lies the Church TELLS Women

J. LEE GRADY

Charisma
HOUSE

10 Lies the Church Tells Women by J. Lee Grady
Published by Charisma House
A part of Strang Communications Company
600 Rinehart Road
Lake Mary, Florida 32746
www.charismahouse.com

Library of Congress Catalog Card Number: 00-109254
International Standard Book Number: 0-88419-737-9

03 04 05 06 — 11 10 9 8 7
Printed in the United States of America

To the most important women in my life:
My wife, Deborah, and our daughters
Margaret, Meredith, Gloria and Charlotte

Acknowledgments

This book would never have become a reality without the prodding and encouragement of three dear sisters in Christ: Joy Strang, Brenda Davis and Maureen Eha. These women, who serve as the editorial staff of *SpiritLed Woman* magazine, challenged me to write what was in my heart, regardless of the criticism that will inevitably come from those who think women belong in the back of the bus.

I also want to thank the many scholars, ministers and authors who broke the theological ground on the issue of women in ministry and helped me understand how to interpret the so-called "difficult" Bible passages that deal with the topic. I am especially grateful to Dr. Fuchsia Pickett, Ruth A. Tucker, Judy L. Brown, Catherine Clark Kroeger, Rebecca Merrill Groothuis and Gretchen Gaebelein Hull. I also want to thank editor Peg de Alminana, whose own study of the original Greek texts added an important dimension to this manuscript.

Finally I want to thank the many "mothers in the faith" who have provided such a rich example for me and who taught me that every man needs input from women of God. Those women include my own mother, Jean Grady, as well as June Leverette (who introduced me to the ministry of the Holy Spirit), Barbara James, Cindy Jacobs, Rose Weiner (who challenged me in 1981 to develop my writing ministry), Alice Smith and the late Carol St. Clair.

Contents

10 Lies

FOREWORD

In the turbulence of the mid-1600s in England, a revival movement began that released women to minister in unprecedented ways. George Fox, the founder of the Quakers, believed that since the Holy Spirit dwells in men and women alike, and since it is He who rightly interprets the Bible, both genders have the same capacity to speak for God.

As a result, early Quaker women traveled the world—sometimes leaving their children for months in the care of their husbands, extended family members or other Quakers—in order to spread the gospel of Jesus Christ. They endured incredible hardship from persecution, often being jailed or even martyred. But their influence was powerfully felt, both within the church and beyond it into society, as they led the way in the abolition of slavery, the fight for women's suffrage and prison reform.

During the next three hundred years God reiterated through other nascent revival movements that He could use women. Methodism, the Holiness Movement, the Salvation Army and the Pentecostal Outpouring each opened the door to women to step beyond the roles of family to impact the church and society.

How was this possible?

History has shown that when a wave of revival sweeps in, those who wholeheartedly pursue God often are carried farther than they ever thought possible. As the Holy Spirit sovereignly moves among God's people, old religious forms lose their power. The evidence of His anointing on certain chosen vessels removes the traditional barriers created by gender, race and age. This makes it possible for God to raise up mighty women such as Catherine Booth, Maria Woodworth-Etter and Kathryn Kuhlman, who, in their determination to obey God, defied the commonly held views of their day regarding women.

Just as these women had a purpose and a call that impacted many for God, so you were created with a unique destiny that only you will be able to fulfill. Along the way you may have lost sight of that purpose. You may have bought into the view that there are limits on what you can do.

Ultimately, what you believe rules you. If you believe your life purpose is simply to fill limited roles, you'll fill them and stop there—never knowing more was available to you. This is what happened to me until God revealed to me the difference between the roles I filled and the calling He had on my life.

As a minister's daughter I grew up serving God. After I married, my husband and I became involved in a vibrant church where we served actively in many different groups—children, youth, singles, music.

Eventually God opened the door for us to begin our ministry in Christian publishing, and since I had a degree in business, I assumed the role of managing the company finances. Because of my position, I began to characterize myself and my ministry in a limited way. "I'm a businesswoman," I would say.

When presented with opportunities for ministry that didn't fit this mold, I was quick to point to someone I felt was more gifted to fill the slot. I believed I was already fulfilling my life purpose. After all, I was a wife, a mother and the chief financial officer in a ministry that was impacting many people for God. I defined myself by my roles.

Foreword

In the early 1990s I became more hungry for God than I had ever been in my life. I sought Him continually. Soon I noticed that my love for Him was contagious, and new hunger was being birthed in those around me.

In that climate God began to speak to me about doing things for Him that were foreign to me—such as mentoring other women and hosting prayer meetings in my home. They didn't fit with my narrow self-concept. Besides that, I *knew* my husband, who at the time was not pursuing God as intensely as I was, wouldn't agree to the new ventures.

One day during prayer, my protests to God about what He was asking me to do were answered by a clear word of correction. "When you stand before Me," He said, "saying your husband didn't agree will *not* be an excuse. You'll be held accountable for what I ask you to do."

I had heard a lot of teaching about order in the home, but I had never heard anything like this. In searching the Scriptures I could find verses only to support and not to disprove it. Romans 14:4 tells us, "Who are you to judge someone else's servant? To his own master he stands or falls" (NIV). I was clearly the Lord's servant and would be accountable to Him. I committed to do *all* He asked of me.

But the more I pursued God, the larger and less comfortable His assignments became. When He first spoke to me about planning a women's conference, I immediately protested, "This must be a mistake. Don't You know who I am? I'm a businesswoman, not a platform minister."

I found that my focus was wrong. As long as I looked at myself—my natural strengths and weaknesses—I wouldn't fulfill what God had for me to do. He was calling me to a new realm, a realm beyond natural ability, that would require total reliance on Him.

The transition wasn't easy.

It might be difficult for you, too. Voices may rise up to reinforce your natural view of yourself. People of smaller vision may want to keep you in your place. Even friends or family may reiterate your limitations—sometimes out of fear. Church leaders you thought would be supportive may consider you too radical as you break out of the box of traditional roles. Some of them may try to hold you back by encouraging you to believe the lies Lee Grady discusses in this book.

And the external voices are not the only obstacles you'll face in fulfilling God's plan for you. The internal sound of your own self-doubt will be even louder. But remember: To the extent that you are self-conscious, you are not God-conscious. Don't let your insecurity destroy your faith! Without it, you'll end up in disobedience; you cannot please God without faith. (See Hebrews 11:6.)

As I obeyed God and moved out beyond my comfort zone, the Holy Spirit led me step by step on a path that ultimately has ministered to thousands through conferences and *SpiritLed Woman* magazine. He has given me assignments that in the natural I didn't understand, but when I have leaned on Him to fulfill them, He has allowed me to bear great fruit.

I feel even less prepared now to do the things He is asking of me, but I know that I can trust Him and that He can use the foolish and simple things for His glory. (See 1 Corinthians 1:27–28.) You can trust Him also. If you continue to say yes to Him in the face of every obstacle, He will work out His pleasure and will in your life. (See Philippians 2:13.)

In the Book of Acts, we are told that in the last days there will be a great outpouring of the Spirit of God that will transcend gender and age: "'And it shall be in the last days,' God says, 'That I will pour forth of My Spirit upon all mankind; and your sons and your daughters shall prophesy, and your young men shall see visions, and your old men shall dream dreams'" (2:17). I believe we are in that day. God is opening the door for you, as a woman, to move into all that He is calling you to do.

However, there will be a price for you to pay when you obey God. In stepping out, you may have to endure the hardship, misunderstanding and criticism that come from facing the erroneous views of women this book addresses. These views, based on invalid interpretations of Scripture, may be used to keep you from obeying God at home and in the church.

Your first line of defense will be to educate yourself by learning the truth—and by understanding that when God reveals truth, it isn't for the purpose of using it as a club to beat those who disagree but to bring you into freedom. When you read *10 Lies the Church Tells Women* and see that some of the things you have been told or taught by the church are based on a wrong analysis of God's Word, you will be better prepared to fully embrace the truth that "there is neither male nor female" in Christ (Gal. 3:28).

In the end the rewards will be worth the price you pay to follow God. You'll have His pleasure in your obedience, the blessing of His presence and the eternal fruit borne out of a life that is wholly devoted to Him.

—Joy Strang, Publisher
SpiritLed Woman magazine

10 Lies

PREFACE

It is written in God's Word that you will know the truth and the truth will make you free. (See John 8:31–34.) The only way we will be able to see God deliver His people from "the ten lies the church tells women" is to learn the truth of God's Word.

The Holy Spirit showed me five things God must set the church free from in order for the revival that we are expecting to come. They are *tradition, prejudice, custom, culture* and *denomination-alism.* The Holy Spirit spoke to my heart that when the church is set free from these bondages, revival will come, and no man, no demon, no devil and no denomination will ever dam it up again. The ten lies discussed so excellently in these pages have helped create these bondages and have kept the church back from the unity that will bring the great revival and the revelation of God's glory.

When God made mankind, He called *them* Adam—the man and woman together. When He took woman from the side of Adam, He meant for her to walk with Adam in harmony, not to be either subservient or superior to him. It was after the Fall that God said fallen man would rule over woman. That was not God's original intent, though it has become "church doctrine." Redeemed man will once again walk with redeemed woman in the way God intended, "submitting themselves to one another" as the Scriptures teach.

Lee Grady has done his homework on this timely and much-needed subject. I believe God has raised him up as a man with an anointed revelation of God's Word, without prejudice, who will write the full truth as the Lord has revealed it. The result is a masterpiece that will allow truth to break all kinds of prejudice and help cleanse the church of all that is keeping the "knowledge of the glory of the LORD" from covering the earth "as the waters cover the sea" (Hab. 2:14). May you read it prayerfully with an honest heart and allow the Holy Spirit to make you free.

—DR. FUCHSIA PICKETT
BLOUNTSVILLE, TENNESSEE

No church that is acquainted with the Holy Ghost will object to the public ministry of women. We know of scores of women who can preach the gospel with a clearness, a power, and an efficiency seldom equaled by men. Sisters, let the Holy Ghost fill, call and anoint you to preach the glorious gospel of our Lord.[1]

—SETH COOK REES
PRESIDENT OF THE PILGRIM HOLINESS CHURCH FROM 1897 TO 1905

And it will come about after this that I will pour out My Spirit on all mankind; and your sons and daughters will prophesy. . . . And even on the male and female servants I will pour out My Spirit in those days.

—JOEL 2:28–29

[Joel's] prophecy has, as yet, been only partially fulfilled. It is yet to be filled out to the full . . . Only a handful of women, as compared with "all flesh," has, as yet, prophesied. That prophecy must be filled out to the full before "that great and notable day," and those who stupidly hinder that prophesying on the part of women are placing themselves, as it were, across the path of the fulfilment of God's Word. Instead of "hastening the coming of the day of God" (2 Pet. 3:12), they are hindering the preparation for that coming.[2]

—AMERICAN EVANGELIST AND REFORMER KATHERINE BUSHNELL

All my life I have been devoted to the advancement of women in education and opportunity. I firmly believe God has a work for them to do as evangelists, as bearers of Christ's message to the ungospeled, to the prayer meeting, to the church generally and to the world at large, such as most people have not dreamed. . . . Let me, as a loyal daughter of the church, urge upon younger women who feel a call, as I once did, to preach the unsearchable riches of Christ.[3]

—EVANGELIST FRANCES WILLARD (1839–1898)
FOUNDER OF THE WOMEN'S CHRISTIAN TEMPERANCE UNION

INTRODUCTION

Four hours south of Salt Lake City, Utah, Protestant pastor Steven Butt lives in an old Mormon chapel that he recently renamed the Be Free Patriarchal Christian Church. From this stone building in the small town of Circleville, this gray-bearded, forty-nine-year-old minister with three wives preaches a bizarre gospel of polygamy.

Never mind the fact that this is the twenty-first century and that multiple marriage is illegal in the United States. Rev. Butt claims that because Old Testament patriarchs such as Abraham, Isaac and Solomon had many wives, the practice is still sanctioned by God. This self-styled preacher can quote chapter and verse to defend his strange views of male superiority and female subjugation, and his wives, ages fifty-one, forty-four and thirty-four (who have collectively borne him five children), seem to heartily agree with his unorthodox interpretation. In fact, they say they enjoy their cozy family life, although one of the wives admitted that she wouldn't be surprised if her husband came home one afternoon with a younger wife to add to his collection.

"We believe that plural marriage is allowed for in the Bible to meet practical, real needs, and this should be acknowledged by the Christian church," Butt told the Associated Press in January 2000. "Obviously polygamy can't be something that's immoral if God allowed it with these people to whom He showed so much favor."[4]

I didn't invent this weird story. But I mention it to prove that people can twist the Scriptures to make them say just about anything.

We could view Rev. Butt's strange church as an isolated example of a pseudo-Christian cult. It is cultic to be sure, but the sad truth is that many Bible-believing Christians have ignorantly misinterpreted or intentionally misused the Scriptures to justify a prejudiced view of women that is just as misguided as the doctrine Rev. Butt spreads in Utah. Even more sad, many Christian women today—such as Rev. Butt's wives—actually defend these views, either because they are intimidated by a male-dominated religious system that claims God's favor rests only on men or because they have swallowed the lie that tells them they are second-class citizens in Christ's kingdom.

It's time we stop spreading these insulting ideas and quit using the Bible to hold women hostage to a male-centered religious agenda. Jesus Christ came to save, sanctify and empower us *all*—male *and* female—for Spirit-directed ministry. Nowhere in His Word does He endorse the idea that women are inferior to men or that the spiritual gifts and callings of the Holy Spirit are conferred only upon males.

Yet for centuries the church has taught godly women that they must quench the holy fire of God that burns within them. As a result, half the labor force in the church has been sidelined and devalued. And while women have been disqualified from the game and sent to the bench, we men have arrogantly told our sisters in Christ that this is God's perfect plan.

As editor of *Charisma* magazine since the mid-1990s, I have observed these chauvinistic attitudes in many charismatic and Pentecostal churches. In 1999 I began to poll readers of the women's magazine we publish, *SpiritLed Woman*. I was shocked when I began to read the testimonials that poured into my office. Each story reflected how deeply ingrained religious prejudice is in the contemporary church.

- A woman named Ann from Ohio said she was told by her pastor at a former church that she could not conduct any type of Bible study unless a male deacon was present. "And holding prayer meetings without a deacon or pastor in the room was definitely out of the question," she told me.

- Ellen is serving with her husband as a missionary in South America. She encountered rejection shortly after her husband, who is the church's pastor, asked her to speak at an upcoming Mother's Day service. "When one of the mothers found out that I would be speaking, she said that her daughters could not participate if I were to speak," she said. "I felt deeply saddened and wanted to cry because God has gifted me to speak, and He had already given me a message for that day."

  Because Ellen's husband didn't want to offend anyone, he pulled his wife off the program. Today she feels the same type of frustration that many women experience because they know they are called to preach but are never allowed to. "I did speak once in our church," she added, "and more tapes were sold of that message than of any other before. I think it is hard for women of God not to feel oppressed when their gifts are not acknowledged and affirmed."

- Margaret was a long-term member at a Pentecostal church in the Northeast, and she began to sense a strong call to full-time ministry. "As I grew in the Lord, many woman and a few men began asking if I could lead a Bible study," she recalled. "So I went to my pastor and asked. The response was a resounding no. He told me that because I was a woman, I would be very vulnerable to Satan and his tactics if I took this leadership role."

- Nina and her husband felt called to help pioneer a youth ministry in their Southern Baptist church in the Bible belt. Her spiritual gifting was in teaching, while her husband was gifted in music and drama. After leading a successful vacation Bible school program one summer, they approached their pastor about starting a regular youth ministry on Wednesday nights.

"Actually, I was not even allowed to attend the meeting to ask permission," she explained. "But the pastors and deacons told my husband that if we did this, he would have to be the one to teach. When my husband protested, saying that the teaching aspect was my gifting, they told him he should teach anyway and that in time he would become accustomed to it."

After this incident, she was denied any opportunity to teach at the church. In one instance she was told she could not teach the youth Sunday school class because there were boys present. And, she added, "several of the deacons routinely warned the younger men not to allow their wives to be friends with me, since I was a bad influence." The couple eventually left the church and joined one that allowed her to use her spiritual gifts.

- Amy, who lives in Florida and has attended seminary, was told that she could not continue to lead her small women's prayer group unless a male elder from her Pentecostal church was present. She was also told that she could not lead a women's Bible study unless her husband attended each week.

- Mary is an ordained minister who has led an interdenominational women's retreat in Tennessee for seven years, but she has frequently encountered rejection from people who considered her ministry illegitimate. On several occasions men have walked out of church services when she approached the pulpit to speak. "After they left, they told their pastor that I had no authority to speak in the church because the Bible says women should be silent," she said.

Because Mary celebrated communion on the last day of her women's conferences, some of the husbands of the attendees openly criticized the meetings, saying that the Lord's Supper must be administered by male elders. "I also did a Bible study in my home for about a year, and a local pastor called various people who attended and told them it was not scriptural for women to teach Bible studies," she added. "He said God did not approve of it, and if they participated they were in rebellion against God."

- Connie was a member of a Baptist church in northern Indiana. She told me that ladies in her church were advised that women should never teach men. "I also was told by a former pastor that I could not ask questions in Sunday school," she said. "He said I must ask my husband the question, and he will either answer me himself or ask the question for me."*

In my study of gender prejudice, I have identified ten lies the church has told women throughout church history—all with the motive of "keeping them in their place." The statements listed below don't sound like lies to many Christians because we're so accustomed to misinterpreting the Bible to uphold views of male superiority. But they are lies just the same.

Before you read this book, which examines each of these ten lies in detail, test yourself to determine if you have been indoctrinated in this religious form of prejudice. Do you believe these statements are true or false?

1. God created women as inferior beings, designed to serve their husbands.

2. Women are not equipped to assume leadership roles in the church.

3. Women must not teach or preach to men in a church setting.

4. A woman should view her husband as the "priest of the home."

5. A man needs to "cover" a woman in her ministry activities.

6. Women who exhibit strong leadership qualities pose a serious danger to the church.

7. Women are more easily deceived than men.

---

*The names of the individuals polled were changed to protect their privacy.

8. Women can't be fulfilled or spiritually effective without a husband and children.

9. Women shouldn't work outside the home.

10. Women must obediently submit to their husbands in all situations.

Every one of the above statements is false. Yet for centuries the church has taught otherwise because it has been under the power of crippling attitudes of male pride, control and domination. The sooner Christian men repent for harboring these harmful patriarchal attitudes (and the sooner Christian women stop promoting them to each other), the sooner the Holy Spirit can take His rightful place on the throne of the church—so that He can empower all His servants to fulfill the Great Commission.

Some female readers may be thinking at this point, "The church has never lied to me. I've never been abused, mistreated or denied opportunity by another Christian." If that is true, then consider yourself fortunate. But even if you have not encountered the most obvious forms of gender prejudice, you can be certain that this pervasive influence has affected you—even if in more subtle ways. Religious chauvinism has been around since the Fall of man, and it lies like a filthy residue on all our institutions.

At the beginning of each chapter of this book you will read shocking quotes from various theologians ranging from respected church fathers such as Origen and St. Augustine to brave reformers such as Martin Luther and John Knox. These men were greatly used by God, but they nevertheless harbored wrong beliefs about the inferiority of women. Because of their positions as leaders and spokesmen for the church, their views have been perpetuated to the present day. If we are going to advance the church into an era of genuine spiritual revival in the next century, we must break with these unholy traditions and embrace a Christlike view of women that is pleasing to the Holy Spirit.

The sad truth is that the church *has* lied to women about their worth and value in God's eyes. And I don't believe "lied" is too strong a word. One theologian who reviewed this manuscript before publication complained that its title would make the church look bad in the eyes of the world. But I believe the only way we can break with the sins of our past is to admit them. We must repent for gender prejudice. We must take responsibility for the way we have misrepresented God and His Word to women everywhere.

Distorting the Scriptures

History is littered with examples of people who have used the Bible to justify cruelty, injustice or bizarre behavior. Anyone can take one or two obscure verses from Scripture, view them through a cultural lens or mix them with a jaundiced personal opinion and then build a doctrine that is totally contrary to the overall message of the Bible. Consider these examples of faulty biblical interpretation, which have caused unbelievable pain in human history:

- The Crusaders during medieval times used biblical passages about Israel's wars with enemy nations to defend violence against Muslims. (A misreading of certain Old Testament passages can easily provide justification for genocide.) During the Crusades, Christian knights inspired by misguided clergy slaughtered thousands of Muslims and Jews in the name of Christ in their efforts to reclaim control of Palestine from the Turks.

- In South Africa, leaders of the Dutch Reformed Church used passages in Genesis to teach that black people are actually animals, not humans. Then, for decades, they used sermons to support an apartheid system that denied basic human rights to blacks in their country, sending a clear message that "the white man's God" viewed non-whites as inferior creatures.[5]

- In Hitler's Germany, some Christians used the Bible to defend acts of violence against Jewish people—saying that Jews deserved punishment because they were responsible for Christ's crucifixion. Today, members of the cultlike Christian Identity Movement, a racist hate group that has an estimated membership of fifty thousand in the United States, uses a twisted interpretation of John 8:44–47 to suggest that Jews are products of a sexual union between Eve and Satan.[6]

- Before the American Civil War, some sincere Christians used the words of the apostle Paul in Ephesians 6:5 ("Slaves, be obedient to those who are your masters") and Colossians 3:22 ("Slaves, in all things obey those who are your masters on earth") to support the practice of slavery. Later, during the years of Jim Crow laws and court-ordered segregation, evangelical Christians used passages in Deuteronomy to teach that God doesn't want people of various racial groups to associate with one another. Even today, some American evangelicals believe that these passages—which condemn intermarriage with non-believers—are instead prohibitions against interracial marriage.

- Some of the great reformers of the past, as well as modern Bible teachers, have taught that God no longer performs healing or other miracles mentioned in the Book of Acts. This view, known as *cessationism* or *dispensationalism,* implies that the Holy Spirit shut down all signs and wonders in the church after the New Testament was written.

  This teaching, widely promoted in the twentieth century through commentary notes in the popular Scofield Bible, is based on one misinterpreted verse, 1 Corinthians 13:10: "But when the perfect comes, the partial will be done away." Many Baptists and other fundamentalists who have promoted cessationism in the past are realizing today that this passage—which says miraculous gifts of the Holy Spirit will pass away after the coming of "the perfect" (or "that which is perfect")—refers to Christ's second coming, not the canonization of Scripture.

- Many Christian denominations have taken obscure Bible verses out of context to create legalistic dress codes for their members. Until 1993, one Tennessee-based Pentecostal group taught that it was sinful for Christians to wear wedding rings. The group based their prohibition on the apostle

Paul's words in 1 Timothy 2:9, which simply instructs women to dress modestly.

- Several pro-homosexual religious groups today twist verses in the Bible to teach that God condones gay sex. One of them, the National Gay Pentecostal Alliance, uses a flawed reading of 1 Samuel 20:17 to suggest that King David and his friend Jonathan were lovers.[7] Those who interpret the Bible this way disregard a key biblical injunction that flatly condemns homosexual behavior.

Such examples of scripture-twisting may seem extreme. But through the centuries church leaders have distorted the Bible in similar ways to deny women the right to preach, teach, pray publicly, pursue ordination or serve as chairpersons of missions committees. The Bible has been used to encourage women not to pursue careers other than homemaking and to teach that motherhood is a woman's only God-ordained calling in life. Ephesians 5:22 ("Wives, submit to your husbands as to the Lord," NIV) has been used to compel Christian wives to tolerate physical or sexual abuse from their husbands in order to glorify God with submissive femininity.

This is spiritual abuse! Consider, for example, that during the 1800s some Christian men used Ephesians 5:22 to justify the practice of wife-beating.[8] In the late 1800s, when the women's suffrage movement was gaining in popularity in this country, many well-meaning church leaders used 1 Timothy 2:12, "I do not permit a woman to teach or to have authority over a man" (NIV), to oppose giving women the right to vote.[9]

Modern mainstream Christian thinking would never support spouse abuse, nor would it suggest that women forfeit political rights to conform to a patriarchal form of government. Nevertheless, we still use the Bible to minimize women's rights and to limit them from having significant spiritual influence.

It's no wonder that so many Christian women struggle with low self-esteem, depression, eating disorders and compulsive behaviors. It's no wonder that religious homes in the United States are ranked among the highest in incidents of domestic abuse—second only to the homes of alcoholics.

The church has told women that their gifts and spiritual callings are inferior to those of men, and it has cloaked this blatant gender prejudice in lofty religious terminology to make it seem acceptable even to women. Yet the impact on women is real: It makes them feel degraded, worthless and dispensable.

Christian women with hearts to serve God have been told that their unique gifts have no outlet, either in the church or on the front lines of ministry. When the Spirit of God has moved upon them to preach, they've been told to keep their mouths shut. When the Holy Spirit has nudged them to use their leadership gifts or their administrative anointings or their teaching abilities, they've been sent to a back room in the church to fix desserts for the Sunday night fellowship hour. When they've stepped out in faith to make a difference for the kingdom of God through their careers, they've been rebuked for taking on "the man's role." It's time for the church to banish these prideful patriarchal attitudes. We must repent and call women out of the shadows and into the realm of authority God has ordained for all who follow the Savior.

Jesus' Radical View of Women

To find a truly biblical view of women and their place in God's kingdom, the best place to start is by examining how Jesus treated them. Jesus went out of His way to challenge the cultural biases against women that were pervasive in Israel during the New Testament era.

We must understand that in the primitive world in which Jesus lived, women were considered little more than property. They were also viewed as evil, ignorant and repulsively immoral. This was the view taught by Jewish religious leaders, who did not allow women to enter parts of the temple and also segregated them from men in the synagogues.

Rabbi Eliezer, who lived in Palestine in the first century, summed up Jewish rabbinical tradition when he wrote: "Rather should the words of the Torah be burned than entrusted to a woman...Whoever teaches his daughter is like one who teaches her obscenity."[10] Another leading rabbi, Jesus ben Sirach, summed up the Jewish position on women by saying, "He who acquires a wife gets his best possession."[11]

In Jesus' day, women were considered the source of all evil because they represented sexual temptation and the original sin of their forebear, Eve. And because they were valued only for their subservient role as wives and mothers, they were not permitted to be taught by rabbis. Basically, women were inferior servants, and their place was in the field, at the well or in the kitchen. If they ever left their houses, they were expected to be veiled. They were not allowed to talk to men in public (except their own husbands), and they were not permitted to testify in a court of law—since the witness of a woman was considered untrustworthy.

It was into this context that the Messiah came, preaching a message of unrestricted access to the Father's love. Because women in the twenty-first century have basic human rights, we often take for granted the revolutionary aspect of Jesus' bold efforts to elevate women in a society that degraded them. What seems like a normal action to us—Jesus' intimate conversation with the Samaritan woman at the well, for example—was really a dramatic act in a culture in which it was inappropriate for a man to speak with a woman in public.

Jesus welcomed women among His disciples, and He angered other rabbis by breaking this ironclad cultural restriction. With so many instances of Jesus' personal interaction with women in the Gospels, it becomes obvious that He was underscoring an important truth. Consider these examples:

Mary, who sat at His feet. In Luke 10:38–42, Jesus commended Mary for listening attentively to His teaching, and He offered a mild rebuke to her sister, Martha, after she begged Jesus to send Mary back into the kitchen. The radical aspect of this passage, which we often overlook today, is that women were not considered worthy of learning anything in Israel at that time; the rabbis of Jesus' day did not allow women to be taught or to sit at their feet as students of the law.

Jesus' tender words to Mary, with which He praised her for choosing the "'good part'" (v. 42), was a clear signal that He had come to call women, not just men, to be His disciples. Women had a place at his feet, too. And if they were invited to learn from Him, would they not also be commissioned to teach others about Him?

The "sinful woman" who anointed Jesus' feet. The account of the "immoral woman" who anointed Jesus with perfume clearly reveals that Jesus was willing to break with the patriarchal spirit of His day. (See Luke 7:36–50.) While the Pharisees criticized Him for allowing this unnamed sinner to touch Him, Jesus commended her actions and ministered mercifully to her by declaring her sins forgiven.

We do not know whether this woman was a prostitute, a street vagabond or some other social outcast. But we must remember that Jewish men in Jesus' time considered all women to be unclean and sinful just because they were the daughters of Eve. They blamed women for all the sin in the world.

Jesus' acceptance of her reveals that He came to remove this painful stigma. As the second Adam, He reversed the curse that came in the Garden of Eden. And by publicly forgiving this sinful woman in the presence of the men who had scorned her, He demonstrated that He had come to remove forever the guilt and shame that had become the portion of all women.

The Samaritan woman who met Jesus at the well. The fact that Jesus even carried on a conversation with this foreign woman, as recorded in John 4:7–30, is evidence of His radical mission.

It is interesting that this encounter at the well is one of Jesus' only attempts to spread His gospel beyond the Jewish people. The Savior modeled His evangelistic ministry to us by speaking with a woman, and her response was to become an evangelist herself (vv. 28–29). Was this not a clear signal that Jesus had come to send women, as well as men, into the harvest fields of ministry?

Jesus was actually very comfortable around women, and we know He allowed many of them to be part of His entourage and lived off of their financial support. (See Luke 8:1–3.)

The woman who was caught in adultery. Like no other New Testament passage, this story in John 8:1–11 illustrates the hateful, judgmental bias that existed toward women in Jesus' day. The woman's accusers wanted to stone her, without exacting the same justice upon her partner. But Jesus' compassionate defense and His words to her, "Neither do I condemn you," provide one of the most beautiful biblical scenes of the Savior's unconditional love.

And that love was directed toward a woman who had been condemned unfairly by self-righteous men. Standing in the gap for her as a skilled lawyer, Jesus silenced her accusers and listened to the testimony of a woman—testimony that was despised in the courts of Israel simply because she was female. Jesus tipped the scales of justice and showed a group of religious hypocrites how their oppression of women grieved the Father's heart.

All these biblical accounts, and many others, make it clear that Jesus came to redeem women from their sinful condition and elevate them to experience His presence as true followers of the Messiah. The gospel we preach today should have the same effect on the women who hear it.

What This Book Is *Not* Saying

The Lord wants to release women from the lies spawned by gender prejudice. Is it possible that in our lifetime these antiquated religious biases will be overthrown, ushering in a new day of cooperation and partnership in which men and women work together to see a global spiritual revival? That's a dream I ache to see fulfilled—partly because I want my four daughters to grow up in a church that extends to them equal opportunity in ministry.

Because some religious people feel so passionate about gender issues in the church—especially the issue of women's ordination—those who call for equal rights for women are almost always vehemently criticized. The arguments I present in this book are certainly up for debate; I don't claim to know all the answers. But I do want to make it clear that while I am calling for full ministry opportunities for women and for full equality for women in the home and workplace, I am doing this within the boundaries of New Testament truth. For the sake of eliminating unnecessary arguments, please understand what I am *not* saying:

1. I am not denying the unique differences between men and women.

The word *equality* is used often in this book to describe the relationship between the genders. That's because the Bible teaches that men and women are equal in terms of their worth and value to God, their shared spiritual inheritance and their shared role in governing creation.

This does not mean that men and women are not uniquely designed. God created male and female with inherent physical and emotional distinctions, and the New Testament declaration that there is no male or female in Christ is not a biblical endorsement of androgyny. (See Galatians 3:28.) Paul's words in Galatians are a fundamental acknowledgment that while men should be masculine and women should be feminine, a person's gender does not limit him or her from enjoying the benefits of salvation or the Holy Spirit's empowering grace.

2. I am not calling Christians to endorse the secular feminist movement.

Why is it that when someone is bold enough to challenge gender prejudice in the church today, he or she is automatically labeled a radical feminist? Let's remember that Jesus was the ultimate feminist of His day—because He was willing to identify with the plight of oppressed women. He elevated them as no other religious leader has ever done in history.

But Christ's call for gender equality bears no resemblance to the rhetoric of modern secular feminists, who often mix their message of equal rights with an angry attitude toward men and a selfish demand for abortion rights. Jesus taught us that we cannot overcome hate with more hate, and this applies especially when we look at the need for healing between men and women.

However, we must also be careful not to fall in the trap of relegating men and women into stereotypical "roles" that are not biblical. Some conservative theologians today teach that men are called by God to be primary "breadwinners" in the family while women are called by God to be "homemakers." This is an extrabiblical idea based on cultural prejudice. Other theologians actually believe that God created men to be "intellectual" while women were destined to be "intuitive." This is not in the Bible! Yes, men and women have differences, but often the "differences" cited by conservative church leaders are imaginary.

Much of secular feminism is about women hating men. Christian feminism, if we can call it that, is about men and women accepting their God-ordained equality and learning to work in partnership with one another and the Holy Spirit. It does not endorse revenge nor does it give women the right to become angry, selfish or abusive in order to right the injustices of the past.

3. I am not encouraging Christian women to revolt against male leadership.

Gender bias is entrenched in the church, and some Christian women who read this book may become angry when they realize how chauvinistic attitudes have been used to manipulate women into a place of powerlessness. I beg every woman reader: Don't let your anger give place to bitterness or malice. Channel your anger into positive ways to bring about change, reconciliation and constructive debate. Don't react with vengeance toward your husband, pastor or male-dominated institutions. True spiritual liberation is not about overthrowing men or putting women in a place of superiority. It is about freeing God's people to obey the Holy Spirit—who works through male *and* female vessels. Instead, ask the Holy Spirit to heal your own woundedness; then pray for God's direction as you seek to liberate others.

To the men who read this book: I beg you not to be defensive. We have so much to apologize for. Our ancestors used God's Word to subject women to abuse. While I am not blaming male chauvinism for all the world's problems, I am encouraging all men to show true manhood by accepting responsibility for our sins against women.

4. I am not calling for a political movement to place women in church leadership.

We can look at the mainline Protestant church in the United States and see that feminist politics has failed miserably. Mainline theologians have rightly discerned that the Bible does not endorse gender prejudice, but their response has been to institute an impotent, man-made program of affirmative action to place more females in church leadership roles. They have forgotten that God is more concerned about spiritual anointing than about how many men or women are ordained.

Having more women in leadership roles won't help the church if those women are not ablaze with the Holy Spirit. Having more female preachers won't help if those preachers don't proclaim the uncompromised gospel. What we need in this hour are women who have a passion for Christ, who yearn for His presence, who love the lost and whose hearts have been set on fire by His holiness. These are the women who deserve pulpits.

Introduction
Questions for Discussion

1. After reading the list of "ten lies" on page 5–6, discuss which statements troubled you. Do you agree with some of these statements? Explain why.

2. Many times people take one or two Bible verses out of context and twist them to construct a false doctrine. Cite an example of this, and explain how a verse of Scripture was misused.

3. Explain why Jesus' actions toward women during the days of His earthly ministry were so revolutionary for that time period. Which of the four biblical women described in this chapter (Martha's sister, Mary; the "sinful woman;" the woman at the well; or the woman caught in adultery) do you relate to the most?

4. What was so revolutionary about the fact that Mary (the sister of Martha) dared to sit at Jesus' feet and listen to Him? How do you think the Jewish men in the house reacted to her actions? Why do you think Martha wanted her sister to help her in the kitchen?

5. Some of this book will deal with the issue of women in full-time ministry. Discuss how you feel about this subject.

6. If you would like to interact with other women who are studying this book, visit the *SpiritLed Woman* website at www.spiritledwoman.com and click on the "10 Lies" icon. You will find further resources for discussion, answers to tough questions, opportunities to interact with the author and interactive support from others who are currently involved in Bible study groups.

The female is more imperfect than the male.
The first reason is that she is colder. If, among animals,
the warmer ones are more active, it follows that the
colder ones are imperfect.[1]

—GALEN, A MEDICAL "EXPERT"
OF THE THIRD CENTURY

What is the difference whether it is in a wife or a mother;
it is still Eve the temptress that we must be aware of in any
woman...I fail to see what use women can be to man,
if one excludes the function of bearing children.[2]

—ST. AUGUSTINE OF HIPPO (354–430)

Woman in her greatest perfection was made to
serve and obey man.[3]

—JOHN KNOX (1505–1572)

...Woman is defective and misbegotten, for the active
power in the male seed tends to the production of a perfect
likeness in the masculine sex, while production of woman
comes from defect in the active force.[4]

—THOMAS AQUINAS

It is an ascertained physiologial fact that the actual
capacity of the average male brain is considerably greater
than that of the female.[5]

—M. BURROWS, IN A 1869 ARTICLE THAT ARGUED
AGAINST ALLOWING WOMEN TO ATTEND COLLEGE IN ENGLAND

Lie #1

God created women as inferior beings, destined to serve their husbands.

Mission agencies in England told Gladys Aylward that she would never be an effective minister in China. In the 1930s, British women were rarely sent to the foreign field to preach; females could go as missionaries only if they were school-teachers or nurses. Gladys wasn't a teacher or a nurse, but she couldn't resist the call of God. So she raised enough money to buy a one-way train ticket to China, then went there with little money and no knowledge of the language.

Her story, which climaxed with her brave efforts to save dozens of Chinese orphans from invading soldiers during the Japanese occupation, was the subject of the classic 1964 motion picture *The Inn of the Sixth Happiness*, starring Ingrid Bergman. Yet despite the impact Gladys Aylward made on China, and despite the lives she protected from certain death, this humble spinster viewed her work as second-rate.

She once admitted this publicly: "I wasn't God's first choice for what I've done for China. There was somebody else...I don't know who it was—God's first choice. It must have been a man—a wonderful man. A well-educated man. I don't know what happened. Perhaps he died. Perhaps he wasn't willing...and God looked down...and saw Gladys Aylward."[6]

Aylward's humility is certainly admirable. Yet it is sad that she believed her gender relegated her into an inferior category, as if women are God's discount-rate substitutes when His prime, first-choice candidates don't respond. This was also the opinion of Kathryn Kuhlman, one of the most prominent healing evangelists of the twentieth century. She too believed that God commissioned her to preach only because His first choice, a man, did not answer the call.

Although huge crowds jammed municipal auditoriums all over the United States to hear Kuhlman speak and many were regulars at her Monday night Bible studies at First Presbyterian Church in Pittsburgh, she often apologized for the fact that she was female. She assured her audiences that she knew her "place" as a woman, and she begged people not to think of her as a woman preacher even though she performed marriages and funerals (not to mention many documented healings) and was referred to as "pastor" by some of her followers.

Kuhlman made a strange admission when she said, "I'd give anything if I could have just been a good housewife, a good cook. And I'd like to have had a big family. It would have been nice to have a man boss me around."[7]

Did God draft Kathryn Kuhlman and Gladys Aylward into the ministry at the last minute because a man said no to the Holy Spirit? If not, why would these chosen vessels view themselves as second-class ministers? It's because of a lie.

It's a lie that tells women they aren't good enough and they will never measure up to a man's worth or abilities. It's a lie that tells women they weren't created on the same level with men. It's a lie that says God made man first and then created woman as an afterthought. All these lies have been promoted for centuries by religious people.

It is obvious from the words of St. Augustine (A.D. 354–430) and John Knox (1505–1572)—two celebrated fathers of the Christian faith quoted at the beginning of this chapter—that gender prejudice is certainly not a new problem in the church. This is pride in its most insidious form, a religious pride that has been baptized and institutionalized by men who claim to represent God without realizing that their attitudes grieve the Holy Spirit.

A Theology of Male Chauvinism

Although Jesus modeled a revolutionary new paradigm of empowerment by affirming women as co-heirs of God's grace, the church throughout the centuries has not adopted His perspective of gender equality except during rare periods of spiritual revival. In fact, Christian attitudes toward women have in many cases more closely resembled the degrading treatment of women seen in Hindu or Muslim cultures than what Jesus called His disciples to demonstrate.

The Gospel narratives describe Christ's radical acts of liberating women, acts that present a totally new view of women that has never been duplicated by any other religion on earth. But tragically, since the earliest days of the New Testament church, patriarchal attitudes have remained in control, partly because leaders found it easier to live in their traditional ruts than to allow their minds to be renewed by the Holy Spirit, who tells us that "in Christ, there is neither male nor female" (Gal. 3:28).

Jewish patriarchal tradition, which was deeply ingrained in the synagogues of Asia Minor in the first century, infected the church in its infancy and continued the tradition of separating men and women during worship—keeping the educated men apart from the ignorant women. As ecclesiastical structures evolved, we find in the writings of most early church fathers a shockingly blatant prejudice against women—if not outright hatred of them.

Tertullian, a respected church father who lived in the North African city of Carthage in the second century, blamed the world's problems on females, and his opinions were modeled by the earliest followers of Christianity. He wrote: "You [women] are the devil's gateway; you are the unsealer of that [forbidden] tree; you are the first deserter of the divine law; you are she who persecuted him whom the devil was not vigilant enough to attack. You destroyed so easily God's image, man. On account of your desert [i.e., punishment] that is, death—even the Son of God had to die."[8]

Respected church fathers of subsequent eras, including the most revered reformers like Martin Luther and John Calvin, also viewed women with contempt. Not only did they consider women unfit for spiritual service, but they also viewed them as having only a domestic role in life. The theology they concocted said that women were put on earth simply to serve in the home, have sex with their husbands and bear children.

Martin Luther, who was not concerned about sounding politically correct in his views, was insulting when he taught on the role of women. He believed that if women die during childbirth, there is no great loss since women have no real function in life other than to have babies! He wrote: "If women get tired and die of [child]bearing, there is no harm in that; let them die as long as they bear; they are made for that."[9] I doubt any pastor or Bible scholar would have the gall to level such an insult on Christian women today. But similar insults are still repeated regularly.

During the 1800s, when the education of women became more common (until then it was considered improper for women to learn anything other than domestic skills), Christian clergymen who opposed the trend actually taught from their pulpits that women were destined by God to be ignorant—and that as a result, schooling them was contrary to divine order. Some even theorized that females had fewer brain cells.[10]

One such sermon from a British pastor, Dr. David Thomas, delivered in London in 1853, infuriated the co-founder of the Salvation Army, Catherine Booth. She wrote Dr. Thomas a strongly worded letter, rebuking him for his chauvinism and predicting that women would one day overthrow such a theory after they were given equal access to educational opportunities.

Booth wrote: "The day is only just dawning with reference to female education, and therefore any verdict on woman as an intellectual being must be premature and unsatisfactory. . . . A brighter day is dawning and ere long, woman will assume her true position, and rise to the full height of her intellectual stature. Then shall the cherished dogma of 'having a cell less in her brain' be exploded and perish before the spell of her developed and cultivated mind."[11]

Lie #1

Today, one hundred fifty years after Catherine's Booth's prophetic declaration, her words ring true. Women today excel in all disciplines of learning and have made inroads in all professions. Yet the church is still dragging its feet, forever mired in religious tradition. The ghosts of institutionalized male chauvinism still haunt our churches, our Bible colleges and our seminaries, and the David Thomases of our day are still telling women that they are less capable, less spiritual, less qualified and less anointed by God for service.

The underlying idea that women are created by God to serve men as subordinates has produced a familiar subset of lies that have been taught from pulpits and in Sunday school classes—and even in women's Bible studies taught by other women. Perhaps these statements sound familiar to you:

- Women are more fit for cooking, cleaning and childcare because they have a God-given inclination for domestic activities.

- Because woman was created to serve her husband, a godly wife shouldn't pursue a career or place her career ambitions above her husband's.

- Because Eve was "given" to Adam as his sexual partner, it is a wife's responsibility to fulfill her husband's sexual desires even if she does not agree with his requests.

These statements have no biblical basis. And no scientific study has ever proven that women are genetically engineered to be more proficient at mopping floors, ironing clothes or changing diapers. As the father of four girls, I can attest to the fact that my daughters did not come into this world with an innate understanding of how to clean their rooms or make their beds!

Certainly women possess a nurturing and protective instinct that makes them good mothers. But it is a cultural bias, not a spiritual or scientific principle, that women were "made" for the kitchen or the laundry room. This is the most common form of male chauvinism, a burden placed on women by selfish men who want someone to wash their dishes.

In a Christian home where the husband and wife relate to each other as equals and "giving preference to one another in honor" (Rom. 12:10), they will always find a way to share job responsibilities fairly. It's perfectly acceptable if the husband cooks dinner; some of the most famous chefs in the world are men. Millions of American women do "men's chores" such as taking out the garbage, mowing the lawn and making household repairs. Recent childcare studies have shown that even though nature requires a mother to breast-feed her infants, family bonds are healthier when fathers also participate in the care of young children.

Because of personal preferences and physical limitations, there are some domestic tasks women will favor. In fact, many women enjoy fulfilling the role of a stay-at-home mother. But is this every married woman's God-given inclination? Is the role of housewife and full-time mother her only option?

We insult women when we spiritualize condescension by suggesting that God created Eve in order to provide Adam with a maid, cook and laundress. Regardless of how a Christian couple decides to provide for their financial needs or how they will divide childcare and household duties, the important issue is that they listen to the Holy Spirit's guidance and seek His will for their situation.

The essence of this low view of woman is rooted in the misconception that the first female, Eve, was created by God as an inferior creature with deficient physical strength, less astute mental capacities and limited spiritual giftedness and that because of her weakness she was meant to live in a state of subordination to Adam. It is the idea that because Eve was deceived by the serpent, she must forever be punished for her disobedience by living in the shadow of her superior male counterpart.

We must read Genesis 1–3 without the lens of cultural prejudice. When we study the Bible, we must *read it* rather than *read into it*. We will discover that the Scriptures do not teach that women have been relegated to second-class status or that they are destined to live in a state of subjugation. These ideas are not implied in the biblical narrative, so why is this view of women still so pervasive among Christians today?

Lie #1

Was Eve Inferior?

The most insulting position taken by the evangelical Christian community is that the first woman in the Garden of Eden was created as an inferior creature who was placed at Adam's side as a subordinate. This view is taught even in Pentecostal and charismatic churches that claim to empower women for ministry.

We often misread the biblical account of Eve's creation in Genesis 2:18–25, in which Adam is provided a "help meet" (v. 18, KJV). The Hebrew word used here is sometimes translated as "companion" in more modern Bible versions.[12] It is a word that denotes intimacy and partnership. But through the centuries, "help meet" has been wrongly used to imply that Eve was some type of domestic appendage.

The fact that Eve was presented to Adam to *help* him does not make her inferior. On the contrary, God had already said, "It is *not good* for the man to be alone" (v. 18, emphasis added), acknowledging that Adam was in an inferior condition without a mate. In the ideal marriage, a wife is a help to her husband, and he is a help to her in return. He is also her "help meet." Their need for each other and their deep sense of mutual dependence are what make marriage so satisfying.

After Eve's creation, God did not tell her: "You are Adam's helper; I command you to serve him well." She was not created for servitude; she was fashioned to be a co-laborer with Adam so they could rule together over creation, as they were commissioned to do in Genesis 1:28: "'Be fruitful and multiply, and fill the earth, and subdue it; and rule over the fish of the sea and over the birds of the sky and over every living thing that moves on the earth.'"

The command to *rule* was not directed only to Adam. Eve was also commissioned with divine authority. Yet so many Christians today believe that God no longer offers the daughters of Eve a place of spiritual influence. Is it no wonder that the church has struggled to make an impact on society, when we have denied half the world's Christians their rightful place of rulership?

In the account of Eve's creation, we read that after Adam wakes up from divine surgery and realizes his wife was taken out of his side, he announces, "She is part of my own flesh and bone!" (Gen. 2:23, NLT). This was an amazing revelation to the man. He recognizes that she is his co-equal, a perfect and desirable mate. Then the passage states: "This explains why a man leaves his father and mother and is joined to his wife, and the two are *united into one"* (v. 24, NLT, emphasis added).

Throughout Scripture the concept of *union* is the most important biblical theme relating to marriage. The uniqueness of holy matrimony is that a man and a woman can unite in a physical and spiritual harmony that supersedes that which can be achieved in any other human relationship. Marriage is not about who is in control or who serves whom. It is about *becoming one.* But a married couple cannot enjoy this deep level of oneness if the man views the woman as an inferior person.

Adam was made in the image of God. The fact that Eve was taken from his side indicates that she also was created from the same divine essence. In certain pagan cultures in the ancient world, people believed that the gods made man out of divine matter and woman out of animal matter. But this is not the case in the biblical story. Both male and female are the children of God.

Some theologians have taught that since Adam was created first and Eve later, it proves that man is superior to woman. But this is a sexist interpretation that makes no sense unless we also believe that Adam was inferior to the rest of creation—which God made before He formed Adam from the dust of the earth! Eve, in fact, was presented to Adam not as an inferior being, but as the crown of God's creation to bring the man from a state of incompleteness to a state of fulfillment. She was not his superior, but she complemented the man so perfectly that she could stand beside him as his equal.

Theologians have argued that the word *help meet,* also translated as "a helper suitable for him," places woman in a subordinate position in her relationship with man. Yet scholar Rick R. Marrs of Pepperdine University notes that the word *help meet* in Hebrew *is often used for God.* When the Almighty is described as "our Helper," we certainly do not assume that He is our inferior! Neither should we draw this conclusion when the word is used to describe Adam's partner—or her daughters.

Eve is called *ezer,* the Hebrew word for "help," in Genesis 2:18. This is the same word that is used to describe God as a divine help in Deuteronomy 33:7, 26, 29; Psalm 33:20; 70:5; 115:9–11 and 146:5. Because the same word is used to describe God, it cannot imply that Eve was inferior to Adam. We should note that the term "Helper" is also used to describe the Holy Spirit in John 14–16. Is the Holy Spirit inferior to man because He is a Helper? Of course not!

We need to clarify that Eve's subordination to man did not occur at her creation; it was a consequence of sin. God's original plan was not that women would be oppressed, denied opportunities, beaten by their husbands, mistreated, raped, stereotyped, bullied or shamed. God's original destiny for woman—a destiny that was secured by Christ at Calvary—is that she rule on earth through the righteousness of Christ.

Before the tragedy of Adam and Eve's fall, we see them in the Garden as partners in paradise. They had been given an equal level of authority by God over creation, and they lived in a state of intimacy with God and with each other that was untainted by sin. They enjoyed equal access to God's presence, and Eve could communicate with the Lord in the same way as Adam.

Their equality encouraged a perfection in their love for each other. The unusual description of the first couple's relationship in Genesis 2:25, "and they were naked and unashamed" (paraphrased), denotes that their marriage was free from the hidden guilt, bitterness and buried wounds that have the power to destroy human relationships.

But what happened to Adam and Eve's perfect union after they succumbed to temptation? God handed down punishments to the man, the woman and the serpent. For the woman, the curse was pronounced with a sense of finality: "Your husband . . . will rule over you" (3:16, NIV).

In some cases the church has taught that Eve's curse was God's ultimate will for her: From now on, because of Eve's deception, women must be ruled by men as a form of punishment. But this is not the intention of God for women; it is simply the consequence of disobedience apart from redemption!

Yes, women throughout the world are oppressed by men as a result of the fall. Look at any sinful culture and you will find the degradation of women through sexual exploitation, domestic abuse and the lack of political and human rights. But God does not want things to stay this way. He provided a Savior who has borne the curse for us!

Consider the judgment that was placed on Adam. He was told that he would have to toil by the sweat of his brow in the fields. (See Genesis 3:19.) These solemn words refer to the curse of poverty—the tragic economic depravity that rules every pagan culture. But we don't use this verse to teach that abject poverty is God's perfect will for men any more than we believe that because of Genesis 3:17–19, all males should have agricultural occupations.

The curse of poverty on man—along with the curse of oppression on women—was reversed because of the grace that was released into the world by the finished work of the Savior's cross. God's plan to draw all of His fallen creatures back into fellowship with Him through Jesus Christ includes the strategy to restore both *men and women* to a place of rulership that the first couple enjoyed before Eve listened to Satan's seductive whispers. Through the cross, women overcome the curse that befell Eve, and they can once again eat from the Tree of Life.

It is at the Tree of Life, the place of restored relationship and intimate communion with our heavenly Father, that we find woman's ultimate calling. Yet we have tried to define a woman's destiny by the act of disobedience that occurred at the Tree of the Knowledge of Good and Evil. God has offered woman redemption through Christ and deliverance from the curse of sin—yet our tendency is to continue to blame her for Eve's deception. God created woman primarily for fellowship with Him, yet we often try to define her worth and value only in terms of what she can do for her husband.

The lie says women were made to serve men as inferior partners. The truth, as revealed in the Scriptures, is that women were created by God as co-equal, joint-heirs of His grace. The lie says women must find their ultimate purpose in serving a man. The truth says that women's ultimate destiny can be discovered only as they seek to become disciples of Jesus Christ.

Chapter 1
Questions for Discussion

1. Can you think of a recent example of male chauvinism you've seen in your church or in the broader Christian community?

2. God described Eve as Adam's "helper" or "help meet." Explain what you think this means in light of the fact that the same Hebrew word for "helper" is used to describe God.

3. Explain why is it illogical to conclude that Eve was inferior to Adam just because she was created after him.

4. Marriage is supposed to be a union in which a man and woman learn to flow in harmony as one. If you are married, do you feel you and your spouse treat each other as equals? If not, why not?

5. Part of the curse of sin for Eve was that her husband would "rule over her" (Gen. 3:16). Explain why this is not the ultimate destiny for a Christian woman.

*God maintained the order of each sex by dividing
the business of life into two parts, and assigned the more
necessary and beneficial aspects to the man and the less
important, inferior matters to the woman.*[1]

—Early church father John Chrysostom (a.d. 347–407)

*A woman's intellect is normally more feeble and her curiosity
greater than those of a man…Women should not govern the
state or make war or enter the sacred ministry. Thus they can
dispense with some of the more difficult branches of knowledge
which deal with politics, the military arts, jurisprudence,
philosophy and theology… Their bodies as well as their
minds are less strong and robust than those of men.*[2]

—Francois de Salignac de la Mothe-Fenelon, in
The Education of Females, published in the late seventeenth century

*Woman has no call to the ballot-box, but she has a
sphere of her own, of amazing responsibility and importance.
She is the divinely appointed guardian of the home… She
should more fully realize her position… is the holiest,
most responsible, and queenlike assigned to mortals; and
dismiss all ambition for anything higher, as there is
nothing else here so high for mortals.*[3]

—Fundamentalist leader John Milton Williams,
in *Women's Suffrage* (1893), which used the Bible to oppose
the movement to give women the right to vote

*We don't believe there's a place for women elders in the church.
When the apostle Paul said that a woman should not "teach or
exercise authority over a man" (1 Tim. 2:12), he did not follow
that statement with a cultural argument. Rather he went all
the way back to creation to show that women weren't intended
to dominate men. The reasons he gave are that the woman
was created after the man, and that she was deceived
when acting independently of his leadership.*[4]

—California pastor and author John MacArthur,
in a statement on women posted on his "Grace to You" website

Lie #2
Women are not equipped to assume leadership roles in the church.

Too many years have passed for most of us to remember that Christian leaders in the late nineteenth and early twentieth centuries aggressively opposed the effort to grant women the right to vote in the United States. In 1920, Roman Catholic bishops in Massachusetts ruled that women would be considered "fallen" if they entered the political arena. Other denominations passed rulings decrying the suffrage movement, predicting that if women began voting they would forsake their domestic duties and trigger the downfall of civilization.

Some preachers jumped on the anti-woman bandwagon and launched an effort to "re-masculinize" the church—out of fear that women would somehow come to dominate it. One of them, Horace Bushnell, a Congregationalist, predicted that if women started voting, their brains would swell and they would eventually lose their femininity—and their morals.[5]

Evangelist Billy Sunday (1863–1935) was among the leaders of his day who were concerned that the church was in danger of being feminized. In his popular sermons he often criticized what he called "plastic, spineless, effeminate, sissified, three-caret (sic) Christianity."[6] Perhaps this fear of feminization is at the root of modern opposition to ministry opportunities for women. But for the most part, those who fight the idea of women's ordination today are still using the same cultural arguments and misinterpreted Bible passages that were used by medieval church patriarchs. Old lies don't die easily.

This was most obvious in June 2000, when the Southern Baptist Convention (SBC), the nation's largest Protestant denomination, passed a policy that states: "While both men and women are gifted for service in the church, the office of pastor is limited to men as qualified by Scripture." One Baptist leader who opposed the measure, Robert Parham of the Baptist Center for Ethics in Nashville, Tennessee, told a reporter in Orlando, Florida, that the fifteen-million-member SBC "has pulled up the drawbridge to the 21st century and locked its members into a 19th-century cultural castle."[7]

Why is it that the church always seems to be fifty or one hundred years behind the times when it comes to making social progress? Why must we drag our feet so clumsily when the Holy Spirit is urging us to break free from religious traditions that hinder His work? In the 1950s and '60s, when American society was coming to terms with the ugliness of racial discrimination, the white evangelical church should have led the way in calling for justice for our African American brethren. But instead, many white churches opposed desegregation and even used the Bible to fight it.

The same is true today regarding the issue of women in ministry. We live in a culture in which qualified women serve as governors, senators, mayors, university deans, corporate presidents, ambassadors and even military commanders. Women have achieved remarkable status in diverse fields including space exploration, medicine, business and athletics. Yet a majority of evangelical churches remain closed to the notion of a woman assuming the role of senior pastor. As a result the world views the church as ignorant, insensitive and irrelevant. Sadly, we deserve that label.

Did Jesus Believe Women Could Lead?

This strong church bias against women in leadership is peculiar when we examine Jesus' own inclusive attitudes toward the women who followed Him. As we have noted already, Jesus affirmed the equality of women in the midst of a culture that denied them basic human rights. He called them to be His disciples during a time when religious leaders taught that it was disgraceful even to teach a woman.

We read in Luke 8:1–3 that the women who followed Jesus were a vital part of His traveling ministry team. This passage says:

> The twelve were with Him, *and also some women* who had been healed of evil spirits and sicknesses: Mary who was called Magdalene, from whom seven demons had gone out, and Joanna the wife of Chuza, Herod's steward, and Susanna, and many others who were contributing to their support out of their private means.
>
> —EMPHASIS ADDED

These women were not just stragglers who stayed at the back of Jesus' entourage watching Him from a distance while they cooked meals for the men. They were Jesus' disciples in the fullest sense, and we have every reason to believe that He commissioned them to minister in His name.

When Jesus sent the Holy Spirit upon the church, as recorded in the Book of Acts, many of these same women were in the upper room and received empowerment on the Day of Pentecost. Those who were Christ's disciples had been commissioned to go into all the earth as witnesses, but they had been instructed to wait until the Holy Spirit came upon them to empower them to fulfill this commission. (See Acts 1:4–5.) When the Holy Spirit came to fulfill this promise of empowerment for ministry, both men and women—including His own mother—received Him. This was noted by Peter, who then recited the verse from Joel's prophecy: "Your sons *and your daughters* shall prophesy" (Acts 2:17, emphasis added).

If Christ commissioned solely men to the ministry of the gospel, why did He send the power for that mission upon both men and women?

The women in the upper room were not the only women Jesus

commissioned. In the story of His visit with the Samaritan woman at the well (John 4:7–42), we read that after He revealed His true identity to her and she pronounced His forgiveness of her troubled past, she began telling others about Him (vv. 28–29). Here we see perhaps one of the clearest pictures in the Bible of Christ as an ordainer of women.

The Gospel account tells us that after her encounter with the Savior, "from that city many of the Samaritans believed in Him because of the word of the woman" (v. 39). Why would the Messiah send this woman into her village to tell others about His power if He was opposed to the concept of women in ministry?

Even more intriguing, this was the first recorded instance in which Christ commissioned someone to evangelize beyond the narrow confines of the Orthodox Jewish community. To prophetically demonstrate that the gospel would ultimately spread to "Samaria, and even to the remotest part of the earth" (Acts 1:8), He sent a woman evangelist to preach!

We must remember the cultural context of this passage. In Palestine at the time of Christ and indeed in all of the Roman world, women were not considered reliable witnesses. Men were taught that the testimony of a woman was not to be trusted because women were considered ignorant and easily deceived. Yet, to whom did Jesus choose *first* to reveal His resurrection on Easter morning? And whom did He commission *first* to tell others that He had triumphed over the grave? Was it not His brave women disciples who were willing to identify with His death while His male followers hid from their persecutors?

Because of cultural biases, Christ's male disciples did not believe the testimony of the women when they gave the astounding report about the open tomb. Yet Jesus appeared to the Twelve and confirmed the witness of the women, and by doing so He intentionally refuted the idea that women could not offer faithful testimony. Indeed, He affirmed the ministry of the women and challenged His narrow-minded male followers to do the same.

After His resurrection, Jesus said to Mary Magdalene, "Go to My brethren, and say to them, 'I ascend to My Father and your Father, and My God and your God'" (John 20:17). Was He not affirming her as a witness of the gospel? Was she not commissioned by Christ Himself both to *go* and to *speak* for Him? Why then do we deny women the opportunity to carry the same message?

Jesus offered similar affirmation to His disciple Mary of Bethany when she broke the alabaster vial of costly perfume and poured it on His head. (See Matthew 26:6–13.) Although it is not clear in this passage why Mary performed this expensive sacrificial act, it appears that her worship was a heartfelt response to a divine revelation of Jesus Christ as the Lamb of God who would take upon Himself the sins of the world.

Because Mary had followed Jesus so closely, sat at His feet as a student, listened to His teachings and believed He was the Messiah, she realized that He was the Son of God who had been sent to earth to pay the ultimate price of mankind's redemption. Because she understood this, Jesus announced to everyone in the room: "For, when she poured this perfume upon My body, she did it to prepare Me for burial" (v. 12).

We could say that Mary of Bethany is a female counterpart to the apostle Peter, who was commended by Jesus when he received a similar divine revelation and announced, "You are the Christ, the Son of the living God" (Matt. 16:16, NKJV). After Jesus commended Mary for her understanding of His heavenly mission, He said of her: "Truly I say to you, wherever this gospel is preached in the whole world, what this woman has done shall also be spoken of in memory of her" (Matt. 26:13).

In essence what Jesus was saying to Mary was, "Finally someone really understands! One of My disciples really grasps the concept I've been trying to explain! I was beginning to wonder if any of you would figure it out. But Mary understands it. She anointed my body for burial because she knows I will die for all of you as your Savior promised by God. Her eyes have been opened!"

In Palestine's patriarchal culture, no rabbi would have honored a woman in such a way. Most religious leaders at that time spoke only to men, and they certainly did not affirm women as worshipers or students of the Torah. Yet here Jesus paid a woman the highest compliment because she understood His prophetic, redemptive purpose before most of His other followers. How ironic that in an environment in which women were not even considered worthy of being taught—and certainly could not learn theology—a woman was one of the first to grasp the mystery of redemption. This alone is enough evidence that Christ intended women to learn at His feet so they could be equipped to become ministers.

A Gospel That Empowers Women

In conservative Christian circles women are expected to live contentedly in the background—presumably to focus on domestic duties—because this is their humble, God-ordained "place" in life. It's a place of invisible service and of godly but quiet influence over children and the home, or perhaps over the church nursery, Sunday school class or women's Bible study.

Women, of course, are told it is an honor to live in the shadow of their husbands or other male authorities and a disgrace for them to assume a place of significant spiritual authority. But we need to ask: Where did we get this warped idea when it was not the perspective of Jesus Christ, nor is it promoted anywhere in the Scriptures?

The Bible, in fact, contains a rich record of women who were placed in authority by God. We must consider the way God used them before we attempt to pull an isolated Scripture out of context to build a doctrine that restricts the ministry opportunities of women. Consider the following biblical women and the level of authority they were given:

- **Miriam.** There is no question that Moses' sister was considered a leader in ancient Israel. This is confirmed in Micah 6:4: "Indeed, I brought you up from the land of Egypt and ransomed you from the house of slavery, and I sent before you Moses, Aaron, *and Miriam*" (emphasis added). She represented the authority of God to the people in the same way Moses did. She spoke for God. That's why she is described in Exodus 15:20 as a prophetess.

    She is also the first person in the Old Testament we see leading congregational worship. Oddly enough, many churches today will not allow a woman to hold the position of worship leader even though Miriam was a forerunner for this vital ministry.

- **Deborah.** Among the judges of Israel, Deborah was the only one who held the respected position of prophet other than Samuel. She is referred to as a prophetess in Judges 4:4, and her attentiveness to God's purpose and strategy resulted in an impressive military victory for Israel that secured peace for forty years. (See Judges 5:31.) She was married, but her husband, Lappidoth, did not share her position of spiritual authority, and we know little about him. Deborah functioned as a civil ruler and was so respected for her anointing and spiritual insights that Barak, Israel's military commander, refused to go into battle without her.

  Deborah, who is called "a mother in Israel" (5:7), presents an intriguing problem for conservative church leaders today who want to promote the view that women cannot function in senior positions of spiritual authority. She doesn't fit in their narrow doctrinal mold, and that's why we never hear sermons about her. She is an oddity, but we can't ignore the fact that the biblical record affirms her godly leadership as well as her intense passion to see God's enemies defeated. We need more women like her today—women who are anointed with supernatural wisdom and who are brave enough to charge into the enemy's camp with faith.

- **Huldah.** After fifty years of paganism and spiritual adultery in Israel, King Josiah assumed the throne and rediscovered the Book of the Law, which had been hidden in the temple. When it was read aloud, he immediately repented and turned to the Lord, then sent his high priest to seek out a faithful follower of God who could speak for Him. To whom did they turn? To Huldah, a prophetess who obviously had remained faithful to the Lord during one of the darkest periods in Israel's history. (See 2 Kings 22:14.)

  We know little about this woman except that she lived in Jerusalem with her husband, Shallum, and that her prophetic message to Josiah came true. The fact that Israel's high priest, Hilkiah, and his associates sought her out to make their inquiry of the Lord shows that she had earned a reputation for hearing from God. It is odd that a group of spiritual leaders operating under the Old Covenant in Israel looked to an anointed woman of God for advice when some Christian leaders today—in the New Covenant age—would consider Huldah "out of order" for assuming a place of influence in the church.

- **Esther.** Although she did not function in a place of ecclesiastical authority, Esther's life proves that God can and does use women in strategic positions of influence to further His purposes. Indeed, he singled out this young Jewish woman and thrust her into the place of an intercessor and deliverer, not unlike Moses, and her prayers and courageous actions literally saved her people from genocide.

  And like Moses, Esther was a shy person. She was tempted to shrink back from her dangerous assignment, but her cousin Mordecai warned her not to be a coward. He told her: *"If you remain silent* at this time, relief and deliverance will arise for the Jews from another place and you and your father's house will perish. And who knows whether you have not attained royalty for such a time as this?"* (Esther 4:14, emphasis added).

  There are many women today in the church who have been called to act boldly, and they, like Esther, struggle with fear. They are called to preach, and their words hold the power to bring salvation and deliverance to many. Yet how many men in our churches are willing to be like Mordecai, to challenge these women to speak out? It seems we prefer that the women remain silent!

- **Phoebe.** Paul commended this woman to the church at Rome and asked them to "receive her in the Lord" when she arrived from Cenchreae to work among them (Rom. 16:1–2.) Although he refers to her as a *diakonon,* the Greek word for *deacon,* the word is translated *servant* in many Bible versions. But it is more accurate to place her in the category of deacon with men such as Stephen and Philip, for the same Greek word is used to describe them.

Paul's commending of Phoebe to the Roman church is also his way of enduing her with apostolic authority, and he obviously expected the early Christians to follow her instructions when she arrived. Most likely she was not coming to Rome to organize Sunday school luncheons. She was sent by Paul to carry out specific plans, probably related to evangelism and church planting. Let's remember that deacons in the New Testament were often powerful ministers who worked miracles when they preached (consider the example of Philip in Acts 8:5–6). It is entirely possible that Phoebe's ministry was of this caliber.

• **Priscilla.** Along with her husband, Aquila, this woman was a noted laborer in the early church, and it was this couple's influence that helped launch the apostolic ministry of Apollos. (See Acts 18:24–26.) It would be safe to say that they also functioned as apostles, since Paul refers to them in Romans 16:3 as "fellow workers in Christ Jesus." We are told that they had a church "in their house" (v. 5) and that this brave couple "risked their own necks" to save Paul's life (v. 4).

Many scholars note that Paul always uses Priscilla's name first when he refers to this couple, doubtless because her teaching gifts were stronger and more recognized by the early church. If only we had men today who were secure enough in their own giftings to allow their wives to excel beyond them at preaching, teaching or other realms of public ministry!

There will, in fact, be situations in which a woman is called to public ministry or to a position of spiritual authority when her husband is not. There is no rule in Scripture that says women leaders must be married or that their husbands must assume some sort of umbrella of authority over them if the woman functions in this role.

• **Philip's daughters.** We are told in Acts 21:9 that Philip the evangelist had four daughters who were "prophetesses." We know nothing about them, but we can assume that their influence was significant enough to be mentioned in the biblical record. Obviously they were engaged in public speaking, and their words carried the same level of authority as Agabus'—a male prophet who is described in the same passage. Philip's daughters were in essence women preachers who experienced a high level of respect for their spiritual insights and level of gifting.

The term "prophetess" used here is taken from the same root word used in Acts 15:32 to describe two male *prophets,* Judas and Silas. Therefore it is obvious that *prophets* and *prophetesses* have the same function and anointing; female prophets are not classified in a lower category simply because of their gender.

Bible translators have been known to play tricks with words when dealing with gender issues. In some cases, for example, they have translated the word for "deaconesses" as "wives of deacons," when there is no reason to believe these women were in some type of subordinate class. But if we examine the word *diakonon,* there is no convincing case that God created two categories of people: *deacons* and *deaconesses,* as if the women belong in a secondary category. The same is true of prophets. Their gender is irrelevant.

- **Lois and Eunice.** The apostle Paul commends these two women—Timothy's mother and grandmother—for shaping the young man's ministry through their instruction and example. Although it is an obscure passage, it is a crucial one because so many churches today use Paul's letters to Timothy to justify misguided policies that limit the scope of women's ministry. It is ironic that people twist Paul's words in 1 Timothy 2:12 ("I do not allow a woman to teach") in order to make a blanket prohibition against women teaching men, when in 2 Timothy 1:5 he commends Lois and Eunice for teaching Timothy the faith!

- **Junia the Apostle.** Paul's reference to this woman in Romans 16:7 has created quite a controversy in recent years. Because she is referred to as an apostle, Bible scholars and translators have assumed that she could not have been a woman—since females can't possibly function in an apostolic role. For this reason the name is often translated "Junias" or is considered a contracted form of the name "Junianus."

Attempts to change the gender of Junia did not begin until the thirteenth century, after the name became uncommon among Europeans. Anyone in the first century would have easily recognized Junia as a common Latin name for a woman. As to whether she was an apostle, theologian Craig Keener makes this point: "Those who favor the view that Junia was not a female apostle do so because of their prior assumption that women could not be apostles, not because there is any evidence in the text."[8]

There are several other examples of women who held positions of spiritual authority in the New Testament church. Chloe obviously led a church that Paul was overseeing (1 Cor. 1:11), and Nympha had a church "in her house" (Col. 4:15). We can assume that these women held pastoral positions. (Conservative scholars, of course, believe they were simply "hosting" the churches in their homes—and perhaps preparing sandwiches and cookies for the after-church fellowship time.)

Paul also refers to two other women, Euodia and Syntyche, as "women who have shared my struggle in the cause of the gospel" (Phil. 4:3). Like Jesus, the apostle Paul had women disciples whom he trained and commissioned to preach and evangelize on the front lines. Where are the women who "share the struggle" of apostolic ministry today? How tragic that the church in the twenty-first century has not empowered an entire army of women with the authority necessary to take cities and nations for Christ.

Why Were No Women Included With the Twelve Apostles?

Many conservative theologians argue that if Jesus really believed in empowering women for leadership, He would have appointed one or more females to serve among His twelve disciples. It is assumed that since all the twelve were male, only men can occupy the top positions of authority in the church.

But again, we must take into consideration the culture of Jesus' day. Women were not allowed to occupy any positions of authority in first-century Palestine. Jesus challenged the gender prejudice of Jewish and Roman culture by allowing women to follow Him, by recognizing them publicly, by affirming their spiritual insights and by commissioning them to be His witnesses. But many scholars believe that to appoint a woman to serve among the Twelve may have been so radical that it would have put their lives in danger immediately.

There was also a prophetic and symbolic reason why Jesus chose to assemble a dozen male followers to represent Him. Dr. Kenneth E. Bailey, a biblical scholar and expert in Middle Eastern studies, believes that although Jesus had many disciples who followed Him in Judea and who ministered in His name throughout the region of Israel, He chose to empower twelve men as His key representatives because He was making a prophetic statement to the Jewish people—and specifically to the religious leaders of His day. To the Jews, the number twelve represented the government of God's kingdom. It was the number of the tribes of Israel—a number with its origins in the sons of Jacob.[9]

By selecting these men, whom the Bible refers to as "the Twelve," He was saying to the rabbis and Pharisees that He was creating a "new Israel." Even as the twelve tribes crossed the Jordan River from the wilderness and conquered Canaan, settling in the land and establishing the ancient kingdom of Israel, so would these Twelve—representing the new message of salvation in Jesus Christ—establish a new and enduring kingdom that would endure forever.

If Jesus had chosen women to serve in this symbolic group, Dr. Bailey points out, the message of a new Israel would have been confusing—since the twelve tribes of Israel were led by the Old Testament patriarchs: Asher, Naphtali, Manasseh, Gad, Reuben, Simeon, Judah, Benjamin, Dan, Ephraim, Isacchar and Zebulon.[10]

In the revelation of the apostle John, this prophetic imagery is futher developed in his vision of a vast, heavenly city—"the new Jerusalem," which represents the glorious church. In John's vision, we are told that the city has twelve gates that represent the twelve tribes of Israel, as well as "twelve foundational stones, and on them were the twelve names of the twelve apostles of the Lamb" (Rev. 21:14).

By choosing His Twelve, and sending them out as a prophetic witness to "the lost sheep of the tribes of Israel," Jesus was saying to the Jews: "My message is from the God of your fathers. In fact, before Abraham was, I existed. I have been sent by the God of Israel—the God of Abraham, Isaac and Jacob—to call you to a new and living way of salvation. And I will build My glorious church with these new and living stones."

By picking twelve men to serve in this symbolic foundational role, Jesus was not making a sexist statement, nor was He denying women a future role in the building of His church. He was, as He often did in His parables, using prophetic symbolism as a means to reach the Jews with His message.

Who Said Women Can't Lead?

Jackie Rodríguez was a Florida housewife and mother of one small child when she began to accept invitations to preach in churches in her city. Her husband, Nuño, a pastor in Orlando, was baffled by his wife's decision to step out and assume such a high-profile role. But Jackie never once asked for a speaking engagement. Churches called her and begged her to minister.

"I didn't ask to do this," she told Nuño once when he questioned her motives. "I have not once picked up the telephone and called anyone to ask them to schedule me. God is opening these doors."

It was not an easy road for Jackie. In Hispanic culture, where *machismo* is a dominant force, women are expected to function in a purely domestic role. And Jackie soon found that *machismo* is also a powerful influence in Hispanic churches. When pastors heard her speak, they were shocked. She spoke with authority, but they could not reconcile her obvious anointing with the cultural traditions that held a vice-grip on their minds. To them, Jackie was violating an unwritten law of Spanish culture.

"Who do you think you are?" pastors would ask her. "You are coming across too strong. You are a woman!" they would scream.

Some of the Hispanic women also opposed her, but Jackie pressed through the resistance and ultimately gained respect.

Looking back on her earliest years in ministry, Jackie realizes that she had to oppose a stronghold of prejudice. "We Hispanic women have been under slavery," she says now. "The Hispanic pastors told women that they should be quiet. They told them to show up at church and then to shut up!"

Jackie no longer fights this battle every day. In 1999, she and her husband became associate pastors at The Church of the People, a twelve-hundred-member Hispanic charismatic congregation in Mission, Texas, on the far eastern border of Mexico. Jackie began preaching sermons and airing a Spanish-language broadcast, *Waves of Revival,* that reaches thousands in the Mexican cities of Reynosa and Matamoros. She also began broadcasting to the entire region a television program featuring her relevant preaching. And people started responding to her message.

There are some leaders in the church today who would say that Jackie Rodríguez's ministry is illegitimate. If they could, they would yank her off the podiums and platforms where she stands and pull her TV and radio programs off the airwaves because they believe her gender disqualifies her from carrying the message of the gospel. How did they arrive at such a warped conclusion?

The prophet Joel predicted that one day the Holy Spirit would be poured out on the church and as a result, "sons and *daughters* [would] prophesy" (Joel 2:28, emphasis added). This passage clearly indicates that when the New Testament age began, both men and women would be empowered and commissioned to carry the message of the gospel to the world. God's Holy Spirit would no longer rest simply on isolated individuals as was the case under the Old Covenant. In the Pentecostal age, *all* believers—regardless of gender, ethnicity or social status—would have full access to the graces of the Spirit and would speak the utterances of God.

If preaching were to have been limited to men only, Joel would not have mentioned *daughters* in his prediction. He would have said instead, "In the last days, I will pour out My Spirit, and your sons will prophesy while your daughters serve quietly in the background and pray for the men."

That is not what the Bible says. It clearly states that women will preach. They will lead. They will be on the front lines of ministry. Like Deborah, they will take the church into enemy territory and watch as the Lord gives victory. Like Esther, they will not keep silent. Like Phoebe, they will co-labor with apostles to establish churches in unevangelized regions.

If this is the clear mandate of Joel 2:28, why do churches that pride themselves on faithful adherence to a literal translation of the Bible reject it? There is no biblical basis for the popular notion that prophesying or preaching is a uniquely masculine act. Both genders have been called to minister in the Holy Spirit's power, and we grieve Him when we restrict the full release of that power by forbidding women to speak God's Word or use their talents in His service. We will answer to God for limiting His work by restricting the flow of His Spirit through women who have been called to speak for Him.

Over the years I've heard countless arguments used to restrict women from preaching or leading churches. When I was involved with a charismatic campus ministry in the 1980s, the top directors gathered on one occasion to decide what speakers to invite to a conference for Christian college students. All the speakers selected were men. When someone suggested that we invite Joy Dawson, a popular Bible teacher affiliated with Youth With a Mission, the president of the group said it would not be appropriate if Joy preached.

"It will be OK if she *'shares'* the Word," the leader said, "But she can't preach. Women *share.*" The idea was that if women are put in a place of public ministry and are asked to speak, they must do it meekly (or sheepishly) to somehow demonstrate that they are not being forceful in the presence of men. How ridiculous! Perhaps the men are afraid that the women will preach better?

There is no biblical basis for the idea that women cannot raise their voices against injustice, challenge sin in the church or call sinners to repentance. There is no scriptural requirement that when women pray, prophesy, lead worship, teach seminars, establish new churches, start drug rehabilitation centers, minister in prisons or preach sermons, they must do it less passionately than men. Why then do so many Christians, even in the twenty-first century, still believe that women who proclaim God's Word boldly are either "masculine" or "out of order"? On more than one occasion I have even heard ministers snidely suggest that women who preach in an authoritative style must be lesbians—because, they say, they "want to do a man's work."

We need to understand that the Bible does not lock women into the stereotypical mold of silent wimps. In the Book of Proverbs, godly wisdom is portrayed as a fearless woman who stands in the middle of the city and "cries out" with a loud voice. (See Proverbs 8:1–11.) She declares: "To you, O men, I call, and my voice is to the sons of men" (v. 4). Not only does she preach authoritatively, but she preaches to men. This allegorical woman is not leading a women's Bible study in her home. She is evangelizing men in the central square of a major city. Yet how many leaders of major denominations in the United States would tell this woman preacher to sit down and shut up?

Catherine Booth, co-founder of the Salvation Army, was often criticized by the male clergy of her day because she conducted a public ministry and provided strong leadership to her evangelistic organization. Her detractors often used the argument that it was "against nature" for a woman to preach because God created females to be weak, gentle and subservient. Mrs. Booth pointed out in her most famous 1859 treatise, "Female Ministry: Woman's Right to Preach the Gospel," that objections to women in the pulpit were purely because of cultural biases and traditions.

In the rigid Victorian culture that Mrs. Booth challenged, women were viewed as delicate, decorative ornaments. They were honored as beautiful but silent moral examples, and they were encouraged to influence the morals of their nation as long as they did it in appropriate ways—perhaps by ministering to the sick in hospitals or by hosting teas to raise money for charitable causes. Yet Booth forcefully argued that women can and should be trained to preach and lead. They are not, she insisted, just decorations or silent influencers.

She wrote: "We cannot discover anything either unnatural or immodest in a Christian woman, becomingly attired, appearing on a platform or in a pulpit. By nature she seems fitted to grace either. God has given to woman a graceful form and attitude, winning manners, persuasive speech, and, above all, a finely-toned emotional nature, all of which appear to us eminent natural qualifications for public speaking."[11]

It is tragic that eloquent women preachers like Catherine Booth had to defend their skills and anointing to clergy in the nineteenth century. It is even more tragic that equally anointed women preachers today must continue to defend themselves. When are we going to stop quenching the Holy Spirit by denying our sisters their right to prophesy? To keep them silent is to tune out the voice of the Spirit. To reject their leadership is to reject the Lord.

Chapter 2
Questions for Discussion

1. Why is it significant that on Easter morning, the resurrected Christ revealed Himself first to His female followers?

2. Read Deborah's story in Judges 4–5. Why do you think traditionally minded Christians don't preach sermons about this Old Testament prophetess?

3. Based on the writings of the apostle Paul, women in New Testament times apparently served as deacons, pastors and even apostles. If someone challenged these Scriptures and claimed that women were never given authority in the early church, how would you respond?

4. Why do you think Jesus did not appoint any women to be among the twelve leading disciples?

5. Joel 2:28 says that God's "daughters" will "prophesy" in the last days. What does this mean?

6. For years Christians taught that it was not "feminine" for women to speak publicly. How would you respond to this argument?

*Out of respect to the congregation, a woman should
not herself read in the law. It is a shame for a woman to
let her voice be heard among men. The voice of
a woman is filthy nakedness.*[1]

—FROM THE JEWISH TALMUD

---

*Men should not sit and listen to a woman... even if she says
admirable things, or even saintly things, that is of little
consequence, since they came from the mouth of a woman.*[2]

—ORIGEN (A.D. 185–254), THE EARLY CHURCH FATHER

---

*Women have no creative power, inventive genius or
originality. Rather [they are] creatures of instinct and imitation,
beautifully adapted to what nature intended.*[3]

—ANONYMOUS BRITISH DOCTOR, IN AN 1869
PAMPHLET OPPOSING WOMEN MEDICAL STUDENTS

---

*Nowhere was the power of divine healing ever given to be
administered by any woman. Women have their rightful places,
but when you put one in the pulpit it is unscriptural.*[4]

—REV. DALLAS BILLINGTON OF AKRON BAPTIST TEMPLE,
IN HIS 1952 ATTACK ON EVANGELIST KATHRYN KUHLMAN

---

*The creational pattern of male headship requires that women
not hold the formal position of the authoritative public
teaching office in the church, that is, the office of pastor.*[5]

—1985 STATEMENT OF THE
LUTHERAN CHURCH—MISSOURI SYNOD

Lie #3
Women must not teach or preach to men in a church setting.

Anne Graham Lotz has been called the best preacher among evangelist Billy Graham's five children. That's one reason hordes of women began packing twenty-five-thousand-seat civic arenas in the year 2000 to attend her series of Just Give Me Jesus revival meetings. Her audiences heard an articulate Bible expositor whose North Carolina accent, rapid-fire cadence and sweeping gestures seemed eerily similar to her father's. Yet this preacher wears a dress and understands the pain of childbirth. She also amazed TV viewers in May of that year when she clearly explained the plan of Christian salvation on a *Larry King Live* broadcast after King asked her, "How can you be so sure you are going to heaven?"

Suddenly, many Americans were asking the obvious question: Is Billy Graham going to be replaced by his *daughter*?

Lotz is indeed a powerful public speaker, and those who have heard her teach the Bible say she just may be the person God chose to assume her father's mantle. Yet many evangelicals in the United States—including her fellow Southern Baptists—still cannot endorse her anointed ministry. In fact, when she stood to address a group of conservative pastors at a 1988 conference, many of them literally turned their backs on her—and turned their chairs around as well. Never mind honoring her famous father. These conservative ministers could not submit themselves to a woman preacher by facing her![6]

Lotz is not the only Christian woman who has been subjected to public humiliation because she dared stand in a pulpit to deliver the word of the Lord. We are familiar with her story because she is the daughter of a celebrity, but there are hundreds of thousands of women in this country who have similar tales of rejection.

There have even been cases in which women were reprimanded just for being physically near a pulpit. Several years ago, my friend Brenda J. Davis, the editor of *SpiritLed Woman* magazine, was invited to sing at a friend's wedding in New York. Though she and her friends were all members of the same church, the engaged couple had decided to get married at a more traditional Baptist church where their parents were long-time members.

On the day of the wedding, Brenda walked to her spot on the platform—three feet from the lectern—and began to sing, as the pianist played behind her and the bridal attendants took their places near the front of the sanctuary. Suddenly, with no warning, a group of six men in dark suits bolted from their seats in the first three rows and rushed toward Brenda.

"No! No! No!" one of the older deacons said gruffly, interrupting the second line of the song. "We don't allow women in the pulpit! No women in the pulpit! You can't stand here!" The other men, obviously flustered, were waving their hands frantically as they shooed Brenda off the podium to a spot on the side of the sanctuary.

"At first I thought the building was on fire," Brenda told me. "Then I thought they were talking to someone behind me." She stopped her song awkwardly in mid-sentence, and her accompanist abruptly quit playing. Once Brenda had been repositioned and the deacons were seated, the piano music resumed. But Brenda found it hard to smile at the audience, especially when she realized that the bride and groom were mortified by the behavior of the deacons.

These men were incredibly rude, but I'm sure they justified their behavior by citing chapter and verse in the Bible, claiming that God forbids women from holding any position of influence in the church—particularly if that position allows them to teach or preach. In many conservative churches in the United States, that argument is always based on one verse in the Bible, 1 Timothy 2:12. They claim that this command issued by the apostle Paul is universal and must be applied to all women at all times in the most literal sense. But the logic used in this argument is seriously flawed, and the typical misinterpretation of this verse has placed women in spiritual bondage for centuries.

What Did Paul Really Mean?

Before we delve deeper into the specific cultural context of the apostle Paul's instructions, we need to examine 1 Timothy 2:12 closely. And as we do, we need to apply the most important rule of biblical hermeneutics: We must interpret this verse not solely on what it says or on what we think it says, but on what the rest of the Bible says about the subject being addressed in the passage.

People who misuse 1 Timothy 2:12 to deny ministry opportunities to all women at all times usually pride themselves on being so-called biblical literalists. "The Bible says it, I believe it, and that settles it!" they say smugly. But in actuality, taking the Bible "literally" can sometimes lead to serious error.

For example, what if we take 1 Timothy 5:23 as a literal, universal command to the church? In it, Paul tells Timothy, "No longer drink water exclusively, but use a little wine for the sake of your stomach and your frequent ailments." Is this verse to be applied to all ministers of the gospel? Does it give ministers the freedom to drink alcoholic beverages? My Episcopalian friends would say yes, but many conservative evangelicals insist that the drinking of wine or any other alcoholic beverage is sinful. They obviously do not accept a "literal" interpretation of Paul's advice to Timothy in this case.

That's because 1 Timothy 5:23 was not meant to be applied as a doctrinal statement for all churches through the ages. It is not to be used as a rule of medicine or morality. It is a personal message from Paul to his son in the faith, and it gives us a glimpse of the apostle's caring relationship with him.

What about 1 Corinthians 11:5, which says, "Every woman who has her head uncovered while praying or prophesying, disgraces her head"? There are members of some conservative Christian denominations, particularly Mennonites, who take this verse literally and require women to wear a covering or bonnet on their heads while in church. But most Christians today accept the view that this passage of Scripture pertains to a specific cultural issue in first century Corinth and that it is not a universal command.

Many parts of Scripture, of course, are to be applied universally. But in Paul's epistles, often his instructions are offered to bring correction to specific situations that had arisen in the early church. In 1 Corinthians 8, for example, he deals with the issue of whether Christians should eat meat that has been sacrificed to pagan idols. Since we don't encounter such circumstances in modern society, we must be careful how we apply Paul's words when dealing with corresponding contemporary issues.

Let's look again at Paul's words to Timothy and ask some important questions about how literally we are to take his instructions. 1 Timothy 2:12 appears below in several translations:

> And I do not permit a woman to teach or to have authority over a man, but to be in silence.
>
> —NKJV

> I do not permit a woman to teach or to have authority over a man; she must be silent.
>
> —NIV

> I allow no woman to teach or to have authority over men; she is to remain in quietness and keep silence [in religious assemblies].
>
> —AMP

> I do not let women teach men or have authority over them. Let them listen quietly.
>
> —NLT

Now let's use some common-sense logic as we seek to understand what is being said here.

Is Paul forbidding women to teach in any setting? Are his words, "I do not allow women to teach," a blanket prohibition? Does this mean women cannot teach other women? Does it mean women cannot teach children in grade school? If we interpret the Bible properly, by looking at the whole of Scripture, we would have to say that Paul is certainly not making a universal decree about women teaching.

After all, he tells older women to teach younger ones in Titus 2:4. Throughout the Old Testament God commands mothers and fathers to teach their children. The "virtuous woman" of Proverbs 31 is described as having "the teaching of kindness . . . on her tongue" (v. 26). And Jesus' Great Commission—which was given to all His disciples, male and female—commands us to teach His gospel throughout the world. (See Matthew 28:19–20.)

Is Paul forbidding women to teach men? If so, does this mean it is unacceptable for women to teach boys in school? If not, at what age do boys become men, and at what point are women not allowed to teach them anymore? After high school? Does this mean women professors cannot teach college courses because adult males are in the class?

Again, we have to look at other places in Scripture where we see examples of women teaching men. We read in Acts 18:24–26 that Priscilla and her husband, Aquila, offered biblical teaching and correction to Apollos. In 2 Timothy 1:5 Paul commends Lois and Eunice for teaching the Scriptures to young Timothy. If the Bible prohibited this type of teaching, why would the instruction of these women be presented in a favorable way?

Is Paul forbidding women to teach or preach only in a church service? Does his demand for "silence" mean it is wrong for women to share testimonies in church, pray publicly, read Scripture or give announcements? It would seem odd for there to be any speaking limitations on women in church, since we are told that both men and women will "prophesy" in the New Testament age. (See Joel 2:28.) And we have examples in the Book of Acts of women prophets, such as Philip's daughters. (See Acts 21:9.) Also, when Paul gives instructions for the use of prophecy in the church in 1 Corinthians 14, he does not limit the gift to men. In fact, he says, "For you can *all* prophesy one by one" (14:31).

Does Paul mean that women are allowed to speak in church except when they are speaking "authoritatively"? If so, how do we distinguish between authoritative and non-authoritative speech? Is a prophecy authoritative? Is a sermon delivered in a Sunday morning worship service authoritative, but a Wednesday night Bible lesson is not? And who is the judge of a sermon's level of authority?

What about music? Is a song that teaches a truth from the gospel authoritative? If so, it is wrong for a woman to sing to an audience of men since the song is a form of teaching? This seems like a silly question, but there are churches in this decade that limit the gifts and ministries of women in these kinds of ways. In fact, I know of a woman who was told she had to stand with her back facing the congregation when she led worship. If she faced the crowd, she was warned, she would be out of order because she was assuming a position of authority over the church!

Is Paul's instruction a blanket prohibition against women holding any position of authority over men? Does this mean women should not hold political office or be placed in management positions over male employees in the business world? Does this mean a Christian man cannot stay in his job if his boss is a female? (I know of conservative evangelical men who have quit their jobs for this reason!)

Do Paul's words here mean a woman cannot lead a church committee? Or does the prohibition apply only to full-time employees of the church, such as pastors? Numerous women in the Bible, including many in the New Testament church, held positions of significant spiritual authority. So a blanket rule against women in authority does not seem logical and in fact would be unscriptural.

If Paul's words cannot be applied universally, what was the specific situation in Ephesus that required him to write these rather harsh words? To understand them we must consider what life was like in Ephesus in the first century.

Bible scholars have documented the fact that bizarre gnostic heresies were circulating throughout the region at that time, and these false teachings posed a serious threat to the infant Christian churches that were budding in that part of the world. That's why so much of Paul's message to Timothy deals with how to guard against false teaching. In a few instances, Paul actually mentions the fact that women were spreading these dangerous doctrines (1 Tim. 4:7; 5:13).

When Paul introduces his reason for writing this entire book, he says, "As I urged you upon my departure for Macedonia, remain on at Ephesus, in order that you may instruct *certain men* not to teach strange doctrines" (1 Tim. 1:3, emphasis added). What is translated as "certain men" is the indefinite Greek pronoun *tisi*. An indefinite pronoun does not indicate gender. Paul is saying, "Instruct certain *people* not to teach strange doctrines." Later in 1 Timothy, it becomes evident that women were doing the teaching of these strange doctrines, at least in part. A major purpose of this entire epistle was to correct unbiblical teachings being presented by women.

In their excellent book *I Suffer Not a Woman,* Richard and Catherine Clark Kroeger explain that certain cultic worship practices involving female priestesses of the Greek fertility goddess, Diana, had invaded the church of that day. These women priests promoted blasphemous ideas about sex and spirituality, and they sometimes actually performed rituals in which they pronounced curses on men in an attempt to spiritually emasculate them or to declare female superiority.[7]

This teaching most certainly bred unhealthy attitudes among some women in the Ephesian church. These women were completely unlearned, but they were spreading false doctrines, and in some cases they were claiming to be teachers of the law and demanding an audience. They were most likely mixing Christian and Jewish teachings with strange heresies and warped versions of Bible stories. Some even taught that Eve was created before Adam and that she "liberated" the world when she listened to the serpent. Because of the spreading of these kinds of fables and hoaxes, chaos threatened the church.

Some of these rebellious women were actually disrupting worship services so they could teach their strange gospels. Rather than listening to church leaders who had been trained by Paul and the other apostles, these women were pridefully claiming that they deserved the pulpit themselves. In some instances they may have wrested control of the meetings and tried to teach or even perform their rituals.

Paul had to bring serious discipline to the situation quickly or the church would have been infected with a deadly virus. So he forbade these domineering women teachers from spreading their lies, and he commanded all the women in the congregation to be submissive so they could learn correct doctrine. The seriousness of the problem demanded a severe response.

To gain more insight into what was really going on in Ephesus at the time, we need to look closer at the phrase "or to have authority over men." The Greek word for "to have authority over" is *authentein,* and it is the only time in the New Testament this word is used. Normally, the Greek word *exousia* is used for "authority."

Bible scholars have noted that *authentein* has a forceful and extremely negative connotation. It implies a more specific meaning than "to have authority over" and can be translated "to dominate," "to usurp" or "to take control." Often when this word was used in ancient Greek literature it was associated with violence or even murder.

We can assume that because this word is used here, women in the Ephesian church were dominating church meetings, usurping the authority of church leaders and proclaiming themselves teachers when they had never been properly taught. So Paul called for an end to the madness. In essence he was saying, "Enough! I am not going to allow these know-it-all women to teach in your church anymore, nor I am allowing them to overthrow or usurp the authority of the leaders I appointed to teach you."[8]

Paul's decree was not so much about the gender of those who were usurping authority but about the fact that they were not trained to teach and yet were pretending to be experts on

Christian doctrine. In fact, Paul uses equally strong words when he warns Timothy about the men who were spreading false doctrines in Ephesus. He tells Timothy that he has "delivered over to Satan" two men, Hymenaeus and Alexander (1 Tim. 1:20), because they were spreading blasphemous heresies.

In Titus 1:10−11, the same solution was given by Paul to men who were spreading false teachings. "For there are many rebellious men...who must be silenced." Yet, we would never generalize these instructions to say that because male false teachers were spreading heresies, then all male teachers must be silenced.

In his day, Paul would have been thrilled to have more skilled *men and women* who could teach the truth! A few women did serve as part of his apostolic team, such as Phoebe (Rom. 16:1), Priscilla (v. 3, NKJV) and Junia (v. 7, NKJV). But in the early church period most women were uneducated. We will discover that Paul's desire for women to "receive instruction" in 1 Timothy 2:11 was actually a liberating message to first-century women—because they lived at a time when Jewish rabbis and Greek philosophers taught that women were not worthy of learning anything.

Aren't Women Supposed to Be Silent?

Although the Bible is full of accounts of women who taught, prophesied and delivered messages from God, many churches today teach that women cannot minister publicly—or hold positions as priests or pastors—because the apostle Paul supposedly issued a universal command telling women to be "silent." The verse most often cited is 1 Corinthians 14:34−35, which says:

> Let the women keep silent in the churches; for they are not permitted to speak, but let them subject themselves, just as the Law also says. And if they desire to learn anything, let them ask their own husbands at home; for it is improper for a woman to speak in church.

But we must remember that in Greek and Middle Eastern culture during the first century, women did not have educational opportunities, and in fact it was considered disgraceful for them to learn. Greek philosophers, including Aristotle, held the view that women were ignorant, unteachable and distracting because of their sexuality.

But the Christian message burst on the scene in Greece with a radical new idea that was best summarized by Paul in Galatians 3:28: "There is neither Jew nor Greek, there is neither slave nor free man, *there is neither male nor female*; for you are all one in Christ Jesus" (emphasis added). Because of the gospel, women were truly liberated from the curse of subjugation that had resulted from the Fall. They were no longer to be viewed as sex objects or as ignorant inferiors or as the property of their fathers or husbands. Along with men, they were called to be disciples of Christ. They too were called to learn at the feet of Jesus.

Paul calls on women to learn the Scriptures "quietly" and "with entire submissiveness." (See 1 Timothy 2:11–12.) They are also commanded to be "silent" in 1 Corinthians 14:34. Obviously, from what we know of the message of the entire Bible, this is not intended to be a universal command to keep women's mouths shut at all times.

We must remember that all Christians—both males and females—are told in 1 Timothy 2:2 to lead "a tranquil and *quiet* life" (emphasis added). Does this mean men are supposed to refrain from speaking? Of course not.

Paul's words about silence are simply calling for *teachableness* in his new female followers. Because women had not been trained to understand the Scriptures (in fact, they had been denied this opportunity!), he was calling them to embrace the discipline of learning the Word of God. In order to become faithful disciples in the true rabbinical tradition, they needed to approach the Scriptures with reverence and a submissive attitude. They could not be disciples if they were know-it-alls or if they opposed God's Word or if they flippantly questioned it. Humility is the only posture a disciple can take if he or she expects to please the Master.

Paul was calling women to listen and to learn. He was not telling them to shut up and be invisible. He was inviting them to enroll in the seminary of the Holy Spirit and to become active followers of

Christ. He was not commanding them to shut their mouths and fade into the background of the church. And if Paul was calling women to learn, then he fully expected them to teach and preach what they had been taught when the process of discipleship was complete.

Again, as we examine the passage in 1 Corinthians 14:34–35 we must look to the whole of Scripture for its interpretation. We know from preceding chapters in Paul's letter to the Corinthians that Paul permitted women both to pray and to prophesy publicly. Just a few verses prior to his statement about silence, in fact, he tells the Corinthians that "all" people in the assembly should desire to prophesy. (See 1 Corinthians 14:1.) He also says that "if *all* prophesy," unbelievers in the assembly will come under spiritual conviction and be converted (vv. 24–25, emphasis added). Paul never limited the gift of prophecy to males.

Therefore he cannot be referring to this type of prophetic speech when he says, "It is improper for a woman to speak in church." He is obviously referring to a type of speech that was creating problems in the church at Corinth. It had created such a disturbance, in fact, that the church's leaders had sought Paul for his corrective advice about the problem.

The Greek word for "speak" in this passage is the present infinitive form, which can be translated "continually speaking up." It implies a type of speech that was disruptive, annoying or shameful. Most likely, there were women in this church who were continually interrupting the teacher to ask questions or possibly to disrupt the meeting or usurp the speaker's authority. Although the Jewish rabbinical tradition allowed men in the assembly to ask questions during a teaching, and the New Testament church continued this practice for all believers, things had apparently gotten out of hand in Corinth.

The Secret to Interpreting 1 Corinthians 14

Actually there is another possible way to interpret this difficult passage about silencing women in 1 Corinthians 14. Many scholars of the New Testament who are familiar with the technicalities of the Greek language insist that part of this chapter is actually a quote taken from another source—a letter written to Paul by the leaders of the church in Corinth. This letter is referred to by Paul in chapter 7, when he mentions "the things about which you wrote" (v. 1). Most of the specific issues Paul addresses in 1 Corinthians, in fact, are topics that were included in that letter.

Paul's seemingly restrictive words about women in chapter 14 take on a different light when we consider that he was very likely quoting a letter from church leaders who were imposing on the young Corinthian congregation a harsh, anti-woman position that was rooted in their rabbinical Jewish traditions. Consider this portion of the passage below, with the quoted section set apart:

26   What is the outcome then, brethren? When you assemble, each one has a psalm, has a teaching, has a revelation, has a tongue, has an interpretation. Let all things be done for edification.

27   If anyone speaks in a tongue, it should be by two or at the most three, and each in turn, and let one interpret;

28   but if there is no interpreter, he must keep silent in the church; and let him speak to himself and to God.

29   And let two or three prophets speak, and let the others pass judgment.

30   But if a revelation is made to another who is seated, let the first keep silent.

31   For you can all prophesy one by one, so that all may learn and all may be exhorted;

32   and the spirits of prophets are subject to prophets;

33   for God is not a God of confusion but of peace, as in all the churches of the saints.

34   LET THE WOMEN KEEP SILENT IN THE CHURCHES; FOR THEY ARE NOT PERMITTED TO SPEAK, BUT LET THEM SUBJECT THEMSELVES, JUST AS THE LAW ALSO SAYS.

35   AND IF THEY DESIRE TO LEARN ANYTHING, LET THEM ASK THEIR OWN HUSBANDS AT HOME; FOR IT IS IMPROPER FOR A WOMAN TO SPEAK IN CHURCH.

36   Was it from you that the word of God first went forth? Or has it come to you only?

37   If anyone thinks he is a prophet or spiritual, let him

recognize that the things which I write to you are the Lord's commandment.

38 But if anyone does not recognize this, he is not recognized.

39 Therefore, my brethren, desire earnestly to prophesy, and do not forbid to speak in tongues.

40 But let all things be done properly and in an orderly manner.

There are several reasons scholars believe that verses 34 and 35 of this passage are quotes from the letter Paul is answering. The most important clue is that the Greek symbol η (with a grave accent) is used at the beginning of verse 36 to signal to the reader that the preceding statement is quoted. Because Greek does not have what we know as quotation marks, this device is used instead.[9]

This would explain why verses 34 and 35 seem to contradict everything that Paul has said up to this point about the full participation of all believers in New Testament worship. The apostle has spent several chapters telling the Corinthians that all can "prophesy one by one" (v. 31). He even stated in 1 Corinthians 11:5 that women can pray and prophesy publicly. So why would he contradict himself in 14:35 by saying that women cannot speak in church?

It is also curious that verse 34 says women are not allowed to speak "just as the Law also says." What law is this verse referring to? There is no law in the Old Testament that says women cannot speak. There is no reference to a Scripture given here. That's because it is not referring to an Old Testament law but to a Jewish rabbinical tradition that the Corinthian church had adopted.

The harshness of the language in verse 35 gives us another clue that this "Law" is actually a man-made rule invented by the same type of legalistic Judaizers that Paul publicly opposed in the churches of Galatia and Colossae. The phrase, "It is improper for a woman to speak in church," can actually be translated, "It is shameful for a woman to speak."[10]

Do we honestly believe this verse reflects the heart of God? Is this the view of the apostle Paul, who ordained women to serve with him in apostolic ministry? It cannot be. Paul is quoting those who held to a degrading view of women—and who actually described women in Jewish writings as vile and disgraceful.

And because Paul opposed this degrading view of women, he responds to the Corinthians in verse 36 with a sharp answer: "Was it from you that the word of God first went forth?" Another translation says, "What? Came the word of God out from you? Or came it unto you only?" (KJV).

This strange response makes no sense if we believe that Paul penned verses 34 and 35. But if he is contradicting the statements made by the Judaizers of Corinth, then we can understand the defiant tone of verse 36. To paraphrase the apostle, he is saying, "What! You are going to silence women when the gospel of Jesus was first preached by women after they saw Him at the tomb on Easter morning? Do you really think the gospel is only for men?"

This passage is one of the most misunderstood parts of the Bible. I believe the only way it can be logically interpreted is to accept the fact that Paul is responding to a quoted statement. This view was repeated by theologian Kenneth S. Kantzer in *Christianity Today:* "In 1 Corinthians 14 we are caught in an intricate interplay between quotations from a missing letter from the Corinthians and Paul's solutions to problems the letter had raised. The verse is clearly not repeating a law of Scripture and cannot be taken as a universal command for women to be silent in church. That interpretation would flatly contradict what the apostle had just said three chapters earlier."[11]

How ironic that we have actually been using a statement written by a group of first-century legalists—men who wanted to burden the New Testament church with stifling Jewish rules and traditions—to shackle Christian women who are called to liberty in the Holy Spirit. Whom do we want to follow: the apostle Paul, who invited women to preach, pray and prophesy in the assembly, or the legalists, who believed that it was "obscene" for women to speak in public?

This verse, so often used to put a bit and bridle in the mouths of godly Christian women, was never intended to keep females from teaching the Bible, proclaiming the gospel or aggressively sharing their faith. How ridiculous! Didn't the Holy Spirit fall on *all* the believers on the Day of Pentecost? On that day, weren't the *women* as well as the men empowered to be witnesses of His resurrection? Didn't Peter remind them of the prophet Joel's prediction that "your sons and your *daughters* will prophesy" (Acts 2:17)? Weren't *all* Jesus' followers—male and female—commanded to go into all the world to make disciples and to teach all nations? (See Matthew 28:19–20.)

We have overlooked the obvious message of the Bible and then taken one obscure passage from Paul's writings and twisted it to keep women in a place of subjugation and insignificance. I'm sure the devil has laughed in delight at the way we have actually helped him silence the spreading of the gospel! By telling women that it is virtuous for them to sit in the back of the church with their mouths closed, we have kept them off the mission field.

Thankfully, women through the centuries who had the fire of God burning in their hearts did not listen to the naysayers who told them they should be quiet. What would have happened if the great missionary Amy Carmichael had been content to stay in her comfortable home in England because of the misguided belief that women are not supposed to speak for God? Because Amy obeyed and preached with fervor, thousands in India found salvation through her Dohnavur Fellowship, and scores of young Indian girls were pulled out of the evil system of Hindu temple prostitution.

What would have happened if Southern Baptist missionary Bertha Smith had adhered to her own denomination's restrictive policies about women in ministry? Because this brave missionary pioneer knew she could not keep silent about her faith, she took it to China and sparked a revival that is still felt there fifty years later.

What if healing evangelist Aimee Semple McPherson had swallowed the lie that says that women should not speak in church? She never would have blazed a trail across the United States in the 1920s with her Pentecostal message, and she never would have started the International Church of the Foursquare Gospel, a denomination with nearly a half-million members in Latin America alone in 1999.

What if the great Bible teacher Henrietta Mears of Hollywood

Presbyterian Church in Los Angeles had assumed that the apostle Paul's words in 1 Timothy 2:12 forbade her from teaching men? She never would have led a Bible study with a young man named Bill Bright, who went on to establish Campus Crusade for Christ and lead an estimated 147 million people to Jesus.

What would the world be like if Salvation Army founder Catherine Booth, healing evangelist Kathryn Kuhlman or Bible teacher Corrie ten Boom had kept their mouths shut when the Spirit of God was prompting them to shout their messages from the housetops? May God forgive us for quenching the Spirit when we have told our sisters they cannot obey His call.

Chapter 3
Questions for Discussion

1. Describe a time when you or someone you know was denied a ministry opportunity simply because she was a woman.

2. Explain why 1 Timothy 2:12 cannot be interpreted literally, without considering the cultural context.

3. Explain why the apostle Paul had to bring correction to the church in Ephesus by asking certain women to stop teaching there.

4. Why did Paul ask the women to be "silent" in the church at Corinth? (See 1 Corinthians 14:34–35.)

5. Explain why it was a radically new concept in the first century for Paul to ask women to learn with a submissive attitude.

6. Some theologians believe 1 Corinthians 14:34–35 is a quote from a letter written to Paul. If this is true, how does this change the meaning of the passage?

*The woman is subject to the man, on account
of the weakness of her nature, both of mind and of body.
Man is the beginning of woman and her end, just as God
is the beginning and end of every creature. Woman is in
subjection according to the law of nature, but a slave
is not. Children ought to love their father
more than their mother.*[1]

—THIRTEENTH-CENTURY THEOLOGIAN THOMAS AQUINAS

---

*[Short hair] is the symbol of the wicked fashion of
rebellion of wives to their husbands' authority or of wicked
daughters who rebel against their fathers. Men wear short
hair as a sign that they take their responsibilities as made
in the image of God and as rulers over their households.
Women are to wear long hair as symbols of their
submission to husband and father, taking their place
with meekness as women surrendered to the
will of God and subject to the authority
God places over them.*[2]

—FUNDAMENTALIST EVANGELIST JOHN R. RICE

**Even the single woman is not to make any decision
without a male head.**[3]

—LETHA SCANZONI, AUTHOR OF
THE 1974 BOOK *ALL WE'RE MEANT TO BE*

Lie **#4**

A woman should view her husband as the "priest of the home."

When Christians twist the Scriptures to make them say what they don't mean, the result is obvious: We invent false doctrines. That's what happened when Bible teachers began promoting the idea that husbands should function as "priests of the home." You can research this in a Bible concordance. The phrase can't be found anywhere in the Scriptures. Neither the Old Testament nor the New tells us that men function as priests by representing their wives to God. But this concept has become a primary focus of modern evangelical Christianity.

As a Bible-believing Christian, Mike* had been taught this idea all his adult life. Since the mid-1980s when he and his wife, Jill,* were married, he continually strived to function as the spiritual leader of his home—and his responsibility increased as each of their four children was born. He believed that in order to be a faithful man of God he must always "be in charge."

Mike also came to believe that if his wife ever stepped into a leadership role of any kind or if her opinions held sway in the home,

---

*Names have been changed to protect privacy.

Satan would be given a license to attack his family. So he insisted on controlling every aspect of home life. Jill was not allowed to pay the monthly bills or handle any aspect of their finances. If the children needed to be disciplined, Mike insisted on spanking them when he came home from work each evening. He made all major purchases—and he got angry with Jill when he discovered that she had bought a lawn chair without asking permission. He insisted on driving when he was in the car with his wife—and even considered it inappropriate for Jill to provide directions.

Mike felt it was his duty to remind Jill constantly that he was the driver in their relationship and that she needed to enjoy the ride. Jill always reluctantly agreed—because she felt God wouldn't be pleased if she didn't respect Mike's headship. She eventually became numb to her husband's controlling demands. Mike was never physically abusive, and his critical comments weren't frequent, but Jill began to feel like a spiritual zombie. Deep down she felt that Mike didn't trust her. And she felt her own desires and dreams were quietly dying.

It all erupted one winter day when their five-year-old son, Tyler,* got the flu. For five days he ran a high fever and had no energy and no desire to eat. In spite of all Jill did to try to strengthen Tyler's immune system by giving him vitamins, the symptoms persisted.

Because Mike and Jill were extremely health-conscious, they always tried natural homeopathic remedies before going to the doctor or taking over-the-counter medicines. But in this instance Tyler didn't seem to be responding to the natural products. So Jill decided to take him to the doctor, and the physician's assistant told her that Tyler had a respiratory infection that might become pneumonia if he didn't take antibiotics.

Jill had the prescription filled and intended to give a dose to Tyler as soon as she got back to the house. But when they arrived and Mike learned about the doctor's report, he told Jill not to give Tyler the medicine. No matter how much Jill pleaded, he refused—saying that the antibiotics might have negative side effects. Jill was so upset and so concerned for her son's safety that

---

*Not his real name.

she erupted in anger and threatened to give the medicine to Tyler anyway. Mike then shot back: "I am the head of this house! You have to do what I say!"

Jill locked herself in her room and prayed as she wept beside the bed. She felt she'd been pushed into a corner by her husband's ironclad demands. Finally she placed the matter in God's hands. It seemed like the only way to preserve her sanity.

The next morning Tyler was so sick he couldn't get up to the table to eat. Jill felt desperate again, so she dared to express her concerns. "Is it right to withhold something from him that you know will alleviate his symptoms and help him get well?" she asked Mike. "Or would you rather watch him suffer while a bottle of medicine is within our reach?"

Mike looked at his wife with resignation and in a restrained tone said, "Give him the medicine." Within twenty-four hours Tyler had improved, and in only a few days he was well. Mike and Jill, meanwhile, were nursing the wounds that had resulted from this quarrel. Mike's pride was hurt because he felt his leadership had been challenged. Jill felt exhausted from having to push so hard to help her son. Their marriage was frayed in the process—and they eventually had to seek counseling.

These kinds of disagreements occur in Christian homes every day. In many cases, husbands and wives who argue over an issue will sit down, listen to each other, calmly try to understand the other spouse's perspective and then decide on a resolution. That's the way conflict management is supposed to work. But domestic strife can't be resolved if the husband believes (1) that he is always right, (2) that it is wrong for him to defer to his wife or (3) that his masculinity is weakened if he admits a mistake. If he believes all three of these fallacies, he qualifies as a first-degree tyrant.

Patriarchs Don't Live Here Anymore

Millions of Christian men today believe their spirituality is measured by the level of firm control they can exert over their wives through "male headship," and they base their beliefs on a wrong interpretation of Scripture. These guys think they are being "real men of God" because they never listen to their wives' counsel or allow their godly masculinity to be "challenged" by their wives' opinions. Where did we get the idea that this authoritarian style of leadership is even remotely Christlike?

The rigid, patriarchal view of the Christian family says that men have been placed in the God-ordained role of full-time boss and provider. The husband's role, according to the conservative religious model, is to lead and protect his wife, while her role is to trust him and submit to his authority at all times without question. Since he is supposedly smarter, stronger and more spiritually capable, the woman has no option but to accept her inferior status.

This view has been derived by misreading the words of Paul in Ephesians 5:23–28:

> For the husband is the head of the wife, as Christ also is the head of the church, He Himself being the Savior of the body. But as the church is subject to Christ, so also the wives ought to be to their husbands in everything. Husbands, love your wives, just as Christ also loved the church and gave Himself up for her; that He might sanctify her, having cleansed her by the washing of the water with the word, that He might present to Himself the church in all her glory, having no spot or wrinkle or any such thing; but that she should be holy and blameless. So husbands ought also to love their own wives as their own bodies.

As mentioned earlier in this book, we cannot understand the full meaning of a Bible passage without reading it in light of its cultural context. We must remember that at the time Paul penned these words (probably A.D. 60), women had no rights in society and were viewed as the property of either their fathers or their husbands. Men considered women to be ignorant (and most of them were, since men didn't allow females to be educated).

First-century Ephesus was steeped in Greek and Roman culture. Greeks viewed women with disdain; Romans taught that wives should stay in their place as inferiors. The Roman philosopher Plutarch believed that women "ought to do their talking either to their husbands or through their husbands."[5] The famous statesman Cato once warned Roman leaders in a speech: "As soon as [women] begin to be your equals, they will become your superiors."[6]

In New Testament times, a man's idea of "ruling the family" was to keep his wife shut away in the house to do back-breaking chores, tend the family farm, provide sexual gratification and bear as many children as he wanted so he could have plenty of laborers to harvest the crops. If she died in childbirth, he found another wife. If she didn't please him in bed, he paid a younger woman outside the home to meet his sexual needs. If his wife shamed him, he beat her. If she dared to run away, he found her and beat her again.

Historian Ruth Tucker notes that in Greek society during the New Testament period, most men considered their home-bound wives boring—so they typically sought the companionship of *heterae,* or professional female escorts. "Athenian law of all periods tended to regard the wife as a veritable child, having the legal status of a minor compared to her husband," Tucker writes.[7] There were no laws against wife abuse. And if a man divorced his wife for any reason, she was economically stranded; the law gave her no recourse to claim any of his estate.

Yet when Paul introduced the Christian message to the Ephesians, he came with a radically new model of family that went to the very core of what was wrong with the world: *"Husbands, love your wives"* (5:25). Perhaps we don't realize what a revolutionary concept these four words were in the first century!

It was even more radical when Paul told the men of Ephesus to love their wives "as their own bodies" (v. 28). This meant that men and women were equals. It meant that Christian men would have to break out of their pagan Middle Eastern mind-set and stop looking down on the wives as if they were brainless, inferior animals. Paul's simple words shattered gender prejudice at its core.

And when Paul told the men to love their wives "as Christ also loved the church" (v. 25), he implied something even more revolutionary: Women are just as deserving of the grace of God as men are. We find in these tender verses the bedrock foundation for the Christian idea of gender equality.

Two Kinds of Christian Husbands

Paul was blatantly contradicting the worldly philosophy of the ancient world, which taught that men and women live on two different social strata. In the kingdom of God, Paul declared, marriage is different from marriage in the world. Men don't beat their wives; men don't rule their homes like despots; men don't threaten divorce as a means to manipulate or control. In God's kingdom, husbands treat their wives with respect—yes, even as equals.

Paul was declaring in this passage that men are no longer "over" women. Husbands can no longer dominate their wives or treat them like chattel. Now that Jesus Christ has come, the curse of male domination over females that began in the Garden of Eden has been broken. Women have been restored to a place of respect and dignity! This was good news for the women of Ephesus; it is good news for all women today.

But if this is true, then why does Paul still say the husband should function as the "head" of his wife? (See Ephesians 5:23.) Does this not give him the right to dominate her? That depends on whether we want a Christian model of leadership or a worldly one.

The husband does function as a leader. But the gospel of Jesus Christ—who was the ultimate example of the compassionate "servant leader"—does not allow men to impose their husbandly leadership in an authoritarian way, nor can men view their role as "head" as part of a God-sanctioned hierarchy that places them over their wives to domineer them or to deny their rights.

Ephesians 5 is not about hierarchy; it is about equality. But if we read Paul's words through a warped lens, it's easy to impose our own misconceptions about male-female relationships on the text. That's why we need the Holy Spirit to help us when we read the Scriptures.

Rebecca Merrill Groothuis, in her book *Good News for Women,* explains that there are really two kinds of male headship from which to choose. One is what she calls "life-giving headship," which was instituted by God in the Garden of Eden when He took Eve out of Adam's side. The opposing model is what she refers to as "ruling headship," which began with the Fall when man and woman came under the curse of sin. Christian men today often view ruling headship as the godly way to lead a family—but it is the wrong model.

Writes Groothuis: "The biblical headship of the husband described in Ephesians 5 is redemptive, in that it mitigates the effect of the fall which places the woman under male rule, and it helps to reinstate woman in her creational place of cultural responsibility alongside man. In life-giving headship, the social privilege and power of maleness is shared by the husband with the wife, and utilized by him according to the terms of love rather than of male conquest and demand. By recognizing her personal and spiritual equality with him, and by putting all that he has and is at her disposal, a husband undoes the male rulership of the fall and, by God's grace, saves his wife from its effects."[8]

In other words, true biblical headship in marriage can be seen only when the husband (1) recognizes that his wife is his equal, (2) loves her sacrificially and (3) empowers his wife by allowing her to share his authority.

Is this not what Jesus did for the church? He condescended by leaving the glories of heaven and taking on the form of a human being. He gave Himself willingly to die on the cross and then bestowed His heavenly authority on His followers, making us co-heirs of His kingdom. This is the pattern Christian husbands must follow. They must humble themselves first by acknowledging that they are on equal footing with their wives. Then they must fully bestow upon their wives the same authority they have—so that together they can rule. This is Christlike headship.

It is a radical concept, and some Christians who have been steeped in the religious tradition of male domination will oppose it violently. Some Christian husbands have made a lifestyle out of being benevolent dictators in the home—and they will most likely quote portions of Ephesians 5 to defend their behavior. Tragically, many women have embraced the idea of being Christian doormats, and they have made their subservience such a part of their identity as women that it has become a place of security for them that they cannot abandon—even though the Spirit of God is calling them to a higher place of liberty.

We Have One Priest

It is true that husbands function in a priestly role in the home when they pray for their wives and family or when they minister the Word of God to them. But we cannot use the "male headship" reference in Ephesians 5:23 to suggest that wives don't also function in this same priestly role at home. Don't wives function as priests when they pray for their husbands? Don't wives teach the Word of God to their children? Can't they also teach their husbands, assuming that their husbands are wise enough (and humble enough) to listen to the rich spiritual insights their wives receive from the Holy Spirit?

Many traditionalists act as if only the husband has full access to God's presence. How ridiculous—and how arrogant! In the throne room of God, His children are not segregated by gender, with men in the holy of holies and women in the outer courtyard. God's grace is made fully available to women and men alike.

The Bible doesn't say only men can understand spiritual truths or receive the Holy Spirit's guidance. When a woman marries, her ability to hear from God is not disconnected. Her authority as a believer in Christ is not surrendered when she recites her wedding vows. Yet this is what we imply when we tell men that they must serve as the sole priests of the home.

Two passages in the New Testament specifically mention the priestly role that a wife can play in her marriage. In 1 Peter 3:1–2, we are told that a Christian woman has the authority in Christ to pull her husband out of disobedience and unbelief. Peter told his readers:

> You wives, be submissive to your own husbands so that even if any of them are disobedient to the word, they may be won without a word by the behavior of their wives, as they observe your chaste and respectful behavior.

Also, Paul told the Corinthians that the woman's authority in Christ can have powerful impact on an unbelieving husband. He writes in 1 Corinthians 7:13–14:

> And a woman who has an unbelieving husband, and he consents to live with her, let her not send her husband away. For the unbelieving husband is sanctified through his wife, and the unbelieving wife is sanctified through her believing husband; for otherwise your children are unclean, but now they are holy.

We should never underestimate the power of a praying wife nor the power of her Spirit-directed words. A woman who seeks God and intercedes for her family will speak with an anointing that can pierce hard hearts with conviction. Through her prayers, souls can be converted, alcoholic husbands can be delivered from their addiction and wayward children can be drawn to repentance. Women can rule with God! Why would we want to deny them this God-given place of spiritual authority?

I would certainly not want my wife to stop praying so that I could fulfill all the priestly duties in my family. The two of us are in spiritual partnership. We are co-laborers in the kingdom, and we are both priests unto God. I expect the Lord to speak to my wife. In many instances, the Holy Spirit has shown her things about our future before He has spoken to me. God has never said to me, "I will reveal My will to you for your family, and then you can tell them what I said." He doesn't speak to me first and my wife later, nor does He limit His dealings with her by speaking "through" me alone.

Back in the 1970s, a large number of charismatic Christians in the United States got involved in what came to be known as the discipleship movement, also known as the shepherding move-ment. The five ministers who led it from their base in Fort Lauderdale, Florida—Ern Baxter, Charles Simpson, Derek Prince, Bob Mumford and Don Basham—taught that every Christian needs a personal "shepherd," an older, more mature Christian who can provide counsel about important life decisions. Everyone involved in the shepherding movement had good inten-tions when they started, but it quickly spun out of control in the 1980s as reports of spiritual abuse became common.

In some churches, pastors told their congregations that they needed to obtain an elder's stamp of approval before taking a new job or relocating to another city. People began to seek permission from their shepherds before making major purchases. A pastor in Virginia told one man in his church that he needed to seek pas-toral permission before having another child; another pastor in Michigan chastised a woman because she received a reimburse-ment check from the Internal Revenue Service and did not seek her shepherd's counsel before spending it. (In many cases these shepherds required their "sheep" to tithe directly to them.)

Many of the people who survived the shepherding controversy without losing their marriages—or their faith altogether—still deal with serious emotional wounds today. Many felt betrayed by spiritual authority; others felt their own relationship with God was stolen from them. By submitting to this form of spiritual abuse, they relinquished the position of access to Jesus Christ that is offered to every believer as a privilege.

Because of the hierarchical structure of the shepherding movement, the sheep were required to go to a man to hear from God. They no longer could approach God for themselves. This often resulted in a sense of worthlessness and shame, and it led to bizarre doctrinal deception because believers started following the teachings of men without listening to the inner witness of the Holy Spirit that is every believer's safeguard.

The shepherding controversy was an embarrassing form of charismatic excess that became cultic. Yet Bible-believing Christians participate in the same type of cultic behavior when they teach that their husbands must function as their wives' priests. They are, in essence, denying women access to God.

Many Christian traditionalists maintain that women should live in the background and allow their husbands to represent them both to the church and to God. They also teach that the husband is responsible for the wife's behavior, as if she were some kind of puppet on a string whom he must manipulate. This is emotionally crippling to women—and it is heretical.

To believe that husbands function as representatives of their wives before God is to believe that women need a mediator other than Christ—and that is the very heresy that sparked the Protestant Reformation! The martyrs who were tortured at the hands of medieval bishops and popes died to defend the doctrine that believers in Christ do not need human mediaries. Why, then, are we promoting today the idea that men must serve as priests for their wives?

The Bible tells us that under the Old Covenant, before the redemptive work of Christ and the advent of the Holy Spirit, God dealt with men through priests. Israel's priesthood represented the people to God and symbolically atoned for their sins by sacrificing animals and offering incense before the holy altar. Of course, their work was simply a foreshadowing of the work of our great High Priest, Jesus Christ. (See Hebrews 8:1.)

Before the coming of the Messiah and the outpouring of the Holy Spirit at Pentecost, God also revealed His purposes through special human messengers who were endowed with a limited measure of the Spirit that enabled them to prophesy and to understand God's will. Under the Old Covenant, God limited His work to these anointed individuals. Yet under the New Covenant, *all* believers have been given the Holy Spirit's power, along with full access to "the spirit of wisdom and revelation in the knowledge of Him" (Eph 1:17, NKJV). We do not have to seek out a prophet like Moses or Samuel to know God's will; we don't have to travel to a special place to find God's presence; we don't have to sacrifice animals to find forgiveness or appear before human priests to obtain cleansing.

Now that Jesus has secured our eternal access into the presence of God, the veil that separated Him from the people has been torn from top to bottom. (See Matthew 27:51.) We have been invited to come boldly before His throne. And, most importantly, we now have been qualified to be priests unto God. First Peter 2:5, 9 says:

> You also, as living stones, are being built up a spiritual house, a *holy priesthood,* to offer up spiritual sacrifices acceptable to God through Jesus Christ.... But you are a chosen generation, *a royal priesthood,* a holy nation, His own special people, that you may proclaim the praises of Him who called you out of darkness into His marvelous light.
>
> —NKJV, EMPHASIS ADDED

Peter does not tell us here that only male believers in Christ are part of this New Covenant priesthood. There is no reference to gender in this passage because "there is neither male nor female...in Christ" (Gal. 3:28, NKJV). Women have been clothed with the priestly garments of holiness, and they have been commissioned to express the authority of His name. No husband has the biblical right to stand in his wife's way, and no wife should dare excuse herself from her higher calling.

Wives Don't Have to Be Wimps

There are, of course, many Christian women who have come to accept the milder, more subtle forms of male domination, and perhaps some of them even enjoy it. They don't want more ministry opportunities, nor do they think other women should push for gender equality. I have heard their arguments often: "I don't want the man's role. My husband provides a spiritual covering for me, and I appreciate it. He's a good provider. I'm glad I have a man to submit to. God speaks to my husband, and I believe I should trust his leadership. God has called women to be meek. I know my place."

It sounds so spiritual! But although it is admirable for a woman to love and trust her husband, submissiveness can actually become a form of idolatry. This happens any time we place a human relationship above our relationship with God. The family is a wonderful creation of God, and we should do everything possible to protect it and enhance it, but we must never love family more than God Himself.

Can a Christian husband become an idol? Yes. Can the ideal of a "happy Christian family" become an idol? Absolutely. How many women have said no to God's will because what He was calling them to do did not match their idea of how a submissive wife should act? How many women have rejected God's plan in order to please their husbands—or their children?

It is tragic that women would sell their birthrights by settling for such a meager portion. God did not call His daughters to be spineless and passive! He did not destine them to be silent when the world is in need of His witness. When the Holy Ghost energizes a woman, she will feel the fire of God as if it were shut up in her bones (Jer. 20:9), and at that point she will feel as though she must preach, pray or prophesy. And we the church must not stand in her way. In this hour, we need a generation of holy women who are so consumed with God's purposes that they will not let anything or anyone stop them.

I'm not calling women to be rebellious or to act superior to men. I'm not inviting Christian women to embrace the anger of the secular feminist movement, which teaches women to hate men and to kill unborn babies. But godly women, like godly men, must be as bold as lions. (See Proverbs 28:1.) Christian women need to start roaring!

Traditionalists will condemn this aggressive form of feminine spiritual zeal as inappropriate. They will contend that women must have a "meek and quiet spirit" (quoting 1 Peter 3:4 as their defense) and insist that God's best plan is for men to be on the front lines of spiritual warfare. Don't believe it! Women have a strategic role to play in the army of the Lord; the men cannot do it by themselves.

Does meekness mean women can't preach passionate sermons or storm heaven with prayer? Does meekness mean women can't lead a national campaign to stop injustice in society? Does meekness mean women can't go to Muslim or Buddhist nations and plant churches—even when it is illegal to do so? Does meekness prevent women from charging into blighted urban areas to set up drug rehabilitation programs, feeding stations and Christian schools to bring social transformation?

Jesus was meek, but He took a whip and drove the money-changers out of the temple. Jesus was humble, but He looked straight into the eyes of the Pharisees and called them white-washed tombs. Meekness has nothing to do with wimpishness, and women of God have not been called to be soft and compliant with the devil or cowardly in the face of spiritual challenges.

The history of the church has been enriched by the lives of courageous women who dared to step "out of their place" in society to serve God. The historian Eusebius recorded many of their stories. He tells of Quinta, a woman who was stoned to death under the reign of the Roman emperor Decius because she would not worship idols; of Potamiaena, who was abused by gladiators and then killed when her torturers poured boiling tar on her body; and of the elderly Appollonia, who was burned at the stake after her persecutors pulled out all her teeth with pliers.[9]

Eusebius wrote of these martyrs: "The women showed themselves no less manly than the men, inspired by the teaching of the divine word: Some, undergoing the same contests as the men, won equal rewards for their valor; and others, when they were being dragged away to dishonor, yielded up their souls to death rather than their bodies to seduction."[10]

Foxe's Book of Martyrs tells us of Symphrosa, who was killed under the reign of Emperor Trajan (A.D. 98–117) because she refused to bow her knee to a pagan god. A Roman woman named Felicitas was beheaded during the reign of Marcus Aurelius (A.D. 161–180), and her sons were also tortured and killed because she refused to recant her faith in Christ. Other women were torn in half by metal hooks, laid on hot coals, burned at the stake, drowned in rivers and even crucified.[11]

Their deaths produced the seeds that gave birth to the bravery of Christian women who would follow. Women like Joan Waste, who was burned at the stake by British Catholics in 1556 because she obtained a copy of the New Testament and memorized large portions of it. Or Teresa of Avila, a sixteenth-century nun who had to hide from her Catholic persecutors because she sought to reform the church by teaching on the love of God. Or Madame Jeanne Guyon, a French Catholic who dared to travel and preach in spite of harsh opposition from her superiors, who told her, "It is the business of priests to pray, not women."[12] Guyon's books were burned, and she spent the last seven years of her life in solitary confinement in the Bastille.

Where would we be today if the brave women of centuries past did not step "out of their place" of passivity to pave the way for the expansion of the kingdom of Christ? What would the world be like if Quaker leader Margaret Fell (1614–1702) had not continued to hold her evangelistic meetings in Boston, even though she was arrested on several occasions and imprisoned for four years? What if eighteenth-century Methodist evangelist Sarah Crosby had not spent twenty years of her life riding on horseback to lead gospel meetings in England? What if nineteenth-century missionary Amanda Smith, a daughter of African slaves, had shrunk from her call to India because her Christian critics told her that women shouldn't preach or go to foreign mission fields?

These women didn't let a man stop them from obeying the

Holy Spirit's call. They didn't need a man to sanction their ministries or represent them before God. And they didn't wait until a male-dominated church asked them to serve the Lord.

I appeal to you, women of God: Let nothing hold you back from fulfilling His call. Don't wait for your husband's permission to pursue God more passionately. Press further into Him, and bring your husband and children with you. Expect to be used by the Holy Spirit to change your world. Dare to ask Him for your holy assignment, and tell Him that you are willing to die to your fears in order to fulfill His mission.

Chapter 4
Questions for Discussion

1. Explain the difference between "life-giving headship" and "ruling headship" in a husband. Why is ruling headship not a Christlike way to exercise authority?

2. Discuss the story of Mike and Jill that appears at the beginning of this chapter. How do you think a woman should respond if her husband has an authoritarian view of male headship?

3. Read Ephesians 5:22–29. Why was this instruction to the first-century church in Ephesus such a revolutionary way to describe the relationship between husbands and wives?

4. Discuss ways that husbands and wives both serve God and each other as "priests." Why is it unhealthy for men to view themselves as the only priests in the home?

5   Peter instructed women to have a meek and gentle spirit. How can women act in this manner and still display courage and spiritual zeal? Do you feel you need to become more bold in your faith? If so, what might be causing you to be passive or fearful?

I am not unacquainted with the word of Paul that women should be silent in the church . . . but when no man will or can speak, I am driven by the Word of the Lord when He said, "He who confesses Me on earth, him will I confess and him who denies me, him I will deny."[1]

—Argula von Grumback (1492–1563)
Bavarian reformer who was imprisoned for teaching the Bible

The rule is express and plain that women ought not to speak in the church, but to be in silence. . . . And therefore they ought not to vote in church matters, besides voting imports some kind of government, and authority and power: Now it is not government and authority, but subjection and obedience which belongs unto women . . . and so is the practice of women among us.[2]

—New England Congregational leader
Richard Mather (1596–1669)

Meetings of pious women by themselves, for conversation and prayer, we entirely approve. But let not the inspired prohibition of the great Apostle, as found in his Epistles to the Corinthians and to Timothy, be violated. To teach and to exhort, or to lead in prayer in public and promiscuous assemblies is clearly forbidden to women in the holy oracles.[3]

—Laws of the Presbyterian Church
enacted by the 1837 General Assembly

Lie #5
A man needs to "cover" a woman in her ministry activities.

Shirley Arnold is a charismatic preacher and Bible teacher who pastors a church in Lakeland, Florida. She spends much of her time ministering in churches and conferences across the country when she isn't teaching or offering personal prayer ministry at a retreat center called The Secret Place, which she established in 1995 for weary church leaders. Although her husband, Steve, has pastored in the past, he currently co-pastors with her and assists her in her traveling ministry.

Back in the mid-1980s when Shirley was an associate campus pastor at Oral Roberts University in Oklahoma, she and her husband were invited to speak in several churches in Romania. This was prior to the 1989 overthrow of the communist regime in that country, and Romanian churches at that time were under severe oppression both from dictator Nicolae Ceausescu's government and from stifling legalistic tradition and religious control. Shirley knew it would not be easy to bring her message of the Holy Spirit's joy and liberty to the Christians there, but she walked through every door of opportunity that opened during the trip.

After she and Steve arrived in Timisoara, they were invited to speak at a large Pentecostal church in the city of Cluj. Never in history had a woman stood in the pulpit of that church. The elders of the congregation sat stoicly on the stage in large, throne-like chairs during the worship service, looking out over a crowd of three thousand desperate people who had jammed into a building that couldn't seat half that many. Shirley wondered if she would be allowed to speak at all, but she made sure she was wearing conservative clothing and a scarf on her head because she had been warned that Pentecostal tradition required this of all women.

"I looked like the proverbial Romanian grandmother," said Shirley, who generally preaches in colorful suits, tasteful jewelry and a contemporary hairstyle when she is in the United States.

The leaders of the Romanian church reluctantly had told Steve that Shirley could give a greeting if he preached. So when the music ended he slyly stood and gave a three-minute-long "sermon"—and then invited his wife to the pulpit to give a "greeting" that included numerous Scripture references and lasted more than an hour. In her bold fashion, Shirley taught from the Word of God through an interpreter and challenged the audience to expect God to do miracles in their midst that evening.

Toward the end of the ministry time, a commotion started in the back of the packed auditorium as worshipers began to bring forward a man who appeared to be crippled. Many in the room who seemed to know the man helped slide him up to the altar area. When he was passed all the way to the stage, Shirley learned that he had been in a serious accident several years prior that left him partially paralyzed. She also was stunned when she noticed that the side of his head was misshapen; a crushing blow had literally bashed in his skull. It was not an attractive sight, but Shirley knew that God wanted to visit this church in power.

As the level of faith rose intensely in the room, Shirley chose to look at the expectant faces in the crowd rather than turning to see the elders scowling on the platform behind her. She stretched out her hand and touched the man's head and asked God to perform a miracle. "It was a high moment in my ministry as I watched that man's skull take a new shape right before my eyes," Shirley told me.

"It was a creative miracle performed right in front of everyone."

Yet after the man stood and was helped back to his seat, Shirley realized that the elders of the church were even more upset than they had been at the beginning of the service. Although they had witnessed the paralyzed man's healing and watched his skull as it was miraculously repaired, they crossed their arms and waited for most people to leave the church. Then they approached Shirley and Steve and filed their complaints.

"You were out of order!" they told Shirley through an interpreter. "God does not permit a woman to minister publicly. God will judge you for this!"

The angry patriarchs then stormed out of the church, leaving Shirley baffled. How could they reject a miracle just because a woman was the instrument God used? She thought of the Pharisees in New Testament times who accused Jesus of being possessed by a demon after He healed a sick person.

Although her encounter with the traditional Pentecostal pastors was not an enjoyable experience, Shirley couldn't help but feel that God had dealt a blow to a powerful religious stronghold at the church in Cluj. It was God Himself who confirmed the message with a supernatural sign.

"I didn't let this intimidate me," Shirley said. "In fact, when we went back to Romania in 1990 after the overthrow of communism, I challenged a group of eight hundred Bible school students to surrender to the call to ministry. When almost all the women in the room stood to answer that call, the men of the school realized it was time for women to assume their positions of spiritual authority."

Crazy Ideas About "Spiritual Covering"

Like the Romanian Pentecostals who denounced Shirley Arnold's ministry, many religious leaders in our country have told women that they are "out of order" or insubordinate if they preach or teach biblical truth—especially if men are in the audience. And in many cases, leaders have innocently twisted various Bible verses to suggest that a woman's public ministry can be valid only if she is properly "covered" by a male who is present. Often women are told that they cannot even lead women's Bible studies or prayer meetings unless a pastor, deacon or some other man can provide proper oversight.

Back in the 1970s, one prominent fundamentalist leader taught that single women must remain under the spiritual authority of their fathers until they marry—even if they are responsible adults in their forties or fifties. This man arrived at his conclusion because of a questionable doctrine of "male headship" that has no basis in Scripture and that has been misused to imply that woman must somehow stay under the authority of a man at all times, whether it is her father, her husband, her brother, a male pastor or some other male relative.[4]

This quirky doctrine—which has evolved into a form of evangelical superstition—has produced some almost laughable practices in the modern church. Some pastors, for example, allow women to carry out almost every imaginable servant ministry by themselves, including secretarial work, childcare, Sunday school teaching and janitorial duty. No oversight is provided for any of these tasks. But if the responsibility includes addressing the church in a public way through teaching, preaching or giving a testimony, or if the task requires the woman to have authority over men, they insist that a man must "cover" her.

One single Christian woman I know felt the Holy Spirit prompted her to organize a special evangelistic activity for children on Halloween as an alternative to trick-or-treating. A creative, gifted administrator, she planned to organize the volunteers for the event, purchase all the candy and decorations, make posters and advertise in local neighborhoods. But before she could begin the project, her pastor came to her with questions. He did not feel it would be proper for her to oversee such an event because she might have to exercise authority over a man without the appropriate "covering."

Another woman I know was told that she could not start a backyard Bible school class in her neighborhood during the summer unless her husband agreed to be present at each session and teach all the Bible lessons. Her church elders said she could plan each day's crafts and make all the snacks, but the "spiritual" aspects of the outreach had to be conducted by a man since he is the proper "covering."

Confusion always follows when this kind of policy is enforced in a church. That's because the "male headship" rule is vague, unwritten and ill-defined—and it is usually applied arbitrarily. For example, during the last two centuries, church leaders who don't allow women to preach or teach without proper "covering" in their local church have sent them to foreign mission fields to pioneer churches, start orphanages or evangelize unreached tribes. The strange rationale used in these situations suggests that God doesn't require the same covering on the mission field since it is too difficult to send a man overseas just to watch the woman work. Does God override the headship policy, then, when it is not financially feasible?

In most cases the "covering" rule simply means that a man must be present when a woman leads a particular spiritual activity—unless, for example, she is teaching only children. Perhaps the idea is that youngsters are not as vulnerable to deception. Or perhaps they don't matter as much to God. This is certainly what we imply when we invent such ridiculous rules.

If a woman preaches to adults, the headship doctrine requires her husband or another male authority to be in the room. If she is not married, another male authority must be present. If she leads a prayer meeting, at least one man must provide oversight, even if he simply watches from the back row.

But does this policy make sense? And does it have any biblical basis? What does a man's presence do for the woman who is ministering? Does the fact that a male is present make the woman's spiritual gifting more legitimate? Does his authority as a man validate her message? Does his presence in the room prevent the woman from slipping into spiritual error of some kind? Does the presence of a man in a room cause the Holy Spirit to favor what is being accomplished? Conversely, does the Holy Spirit withdraw His blessing from a Bible study or prayer meeting if only women are involved in it?

And what about situations in which women minister outside the confines of the church? If a woman senses the Holy Spirit leading her to share the gospel with an unbelieving man in the parking lot at the grocery store, does she need another Christian man to "cover" her while she shares her testimony or reads to him from an evangelistic tract? If she is invited to speak about her faith to a Bible study group in her workplace, should she turn down the opportunity if there isn't a male co-worker available to "cover" her?

How ridiculous that we must even ask such questions in the twenty-first century! Do we not believe that it is the anointing of the Holy Spirit that brings about spiritual results—whether in a church service, at a prayer meeting, in a Bible study or on the streets? If the Holy Spirit's power is necessary to bring about genuine spiritual impact, then what difference does it make whether the vessel He uses is male or female? To say that the presence of a man adds credibility to prayer or Spirit-empowered ministry is to trust in the flesh—a sin that the Old Testament tells us brings God's curse. (See Jeremiah 17:5.)

Does a Woman Need a "Covering"?

There is certainly no verse in the Bible that says, "If a woman teaches My Word, make sure a man is present so she will be covered properly." And there is no passage in Scripture that warns women by saying, "Let every woman be properly submitted to a man so she will not get out of line and lead My people into deception." Nor does the Bible say, "Since man is the head of woman, she cannot minister in My name unless her male spiritual authority is carefully watching every move she makes."

Yet conservative Christians today cite these non-existent "verses" repeatedly when they impose their man-made limitations on women's spiritual callings and ministries. Why do we add words to the Bible to make it say things that it doesn't say?

What traditionalists usually cite, if they use the Bible to support their unbiblical view of "male headship," is two passages from 1 Corinthians 11. Verse 3 says:

> But I want you to understand that Christ is the head of every man, and the man is the head of a woman, and God is the head of Christ.

Then, a few sentences later in a discussion about whether first-century Christian women in Corinth could worship without head coverings, the apostle Paul says in verse 10:

So a woman should wear a covering on her head as a sign of authority because the angels are watching.

—NLT

Interestingly, those who use Paul's words here to prohibit women from ministry miss a key point in verse 5, which states:

But every woman who has her head uncovered *while praying or prophesying,* disgraces her head; for she is one and the same with her whose head is shaved.

—EMPHASIS ADDED

Notice that the apostle here does not attempt to stop the women of Corinth from praying in a public worship service or from delivering a prophetic message from God. The contentious issue being addressed in this passage is not female prophets. In fact, it would seem that Paul is rather accustomed to having women preach and pray in the early church; we know also that Paul had many female associates whom he considered valuable apostolic "co-workers" and whom he commissioned to carry out his gospel ministry. This is why we must conclude that what he is addressing in this passage in 1 Corinthians is not what women can or cannot do in the ministry but *how they do it.*

While we must acknowledge that this is a complex passage to interpret (some theologians rank 1 Corinthians 11:1–16 as one of the top three or four most difficult sections of Scripture in the whole Bible), we can arrive at three simple conclusions after studying it carefully:

1. Women who have been redeemed by Christ don't need a superficial spiritual covering.

Although scholars disagree on the details of the context of this verse, it is safe to say that a dispute had arisen in the Corinthian church over whether women should wear head coverings during public worship. We are not certain what these coverings were. Some scholars suggest they were veils; others say they were similar to the Jewish prayer shawl known as the *tallith*—which men wore to signify both reverence before God and an acknowledgment of shame and sinfulness. Whatever the coverings were, the controversy stirred by them had created ugly divisions in the church, and leaders had appealed to Paul for an apostolic resolution to the matter (v. 18).

Some scholars, including American pioneer evangelist Katherine Bushnell, contend that the real purpose behind Paul's message on head coverings was to forbid the use of them on men. She notes in her 1923 book, *God's Word to Women,* that early Christians took a strong stand against the Jewish practice of covering the head during worship because it was a sign of the guilt and condemnation that Christ came to remove from us. (This practice has evolved to the use of the *yarmulke* by Jewish men today). First-century Jewish believers, by continuing to wear the head coverings, were not acknowledging the atoning grace of Christ's redemption, and this is why Paul says in verse 4, "Every man who has something on his head while praying or prophesying, disgraces his head."[5]

Yet the situation was more complicated for women. Most theologians believe that some enthusiastic women converts had discontinued wearing these head coverings because they had come to understand that in Christ they were free from such legalistic requirements. They were rejecting a Jewish religious code that was still very much enforced in the early Christian church. They apparently understood, and rightly so, that they did not need a head covering to approach God—because salvation cannot be earned through the law. Salvation is the free gift of the Father because of Jesus Christ's obedience on the cross; we cannot earn it by our adherence to religious rules or dress codes.

Yet Paul here calls for propriety and order and seems to be saying to these women that it would be better for them to have their heads covered out of a motive of cultural sensitivity—even though the covering was not necessary to bring them into God's presence or to grant them spiritual favor. Apparently, in Corinthian society, it was considered disgraceful for women to worship without this head covering. In fact, some Greeks associated uncovered women with prostitutes who were known to shave their heads or wear their hair in a wild, loose fashion. Theologian Judy Brown, author of *Women Ministers According to Scripture,* suggests that the covering was designed to hide a woman's hair:

> It seems that a married woman's hair was regarded as such a display of her feminine beauty that it was reserved for her husband's eyes alone. For her to uncover her hair in public was an act of immodesty and a display of disrespect for her husband. Amongst Jews, it was grounds for divorce. An honorable wife would not wish to shame her husband by appearing to be single or promiscuous, so she would be sure to cover her hair properly.[6]

It is also entirely possible that some of the women who were violating this cultural rule were converts who were married to uncoverted Jews. The Christian women, by breaking tradition, were setting themselves up for serious marital strife. Quite possibly some of the women also were flagrantly ignoring their husbands' concerns or even treating them with contempt.

So Paul acknowledges that it would be best for the female converts of Corinth to continue wearing head coverings. Yet in his concluding words on the subject he makes this curious statement in 1 Corinthians 11:13: "Judge for yourselves: is it proper for a woman to pray to God with head uncovered?" Then he says that a woman's hair is "a glory" and "is given to her for a covering" (v. 15), as if to say that her hair is a sufficient covering and should be displayed.

Paul recognizes here that God has already "covered" His daughters. They do not have to live in shame anymore because Jesus has paid the price for their sinful nature. They do not need a prayer shawl to enter His presence. They do not need to hide their hair, since it symbolizes the God-given beauty of their gender. Yet for the sake of cultural sensitivity and to facilitate harmony in a divided church, he asks women to continue the practice of covering their heads even though it is not a condition for God's love and acceptance. With his long-range view into the future, Paul most likely understood that these cultural requirements would change over time and that believers in the future would not have to struggle with this issue.

2. Christian wives are called to show respect to their husbands.

It is interesting that in this deeply theological debate over whether Christian men and women should wear head coverings, Paul inserts several key statements about the way husbands and wives are called to relate to each other. He tells the Corinthians that "the man is the head of a woman" (1 Cor. 11:3) and then adds, "for indeed man was not created for the woman's sake, but woman for the man's sake" (v. 9).

Why would Paul bring these statements into the argument about head coverings? It is most likely because the women who had decided to worship with their heads uncovered were taking their Christian liberty too far. Though they had come to a genuine realization that they did not need to be covered when they prayed or prophesied, those around them who disagreed viewed their decision to pray in an uncovered state as inappropriate and even rebellious. And because uncovered women were viewed as sensual and immoral, and sometimes compared to prostitutes, the husbands of these women were put in a bad position. Their honor and dignity was at stake because of the actions of their wives.

Paul's simple solution, therefore, was to remind these women that they could not act independently of their husbands in the matter. The fact that Paul was forced to say, "Man was not created for the woman's sake" (1 Cor. 11:9) was his way of dealing with an attitude problem in these female converts—some of whom could very likely have been prominent preachers or leaders in the Corinthian church. What he was saying was this: "Hold on! Just because you have the revelation of God's free grace in Christ doesn't mean you can put your marriage at stake to prove it!"

It is important to point out that when Paul says "the man is the head of a woman" (v. 3), it should be translated "the husband is the head of the wife." The Greek word *aner* can be translated either "man" or "husband," and the word *gunaikos* can be translated "woman" or "wife." Paul is specifically dealing in this passage with a situation that involved strained marriages. He is not, as some church leaders have wrongly taught, promoting the idea that *all* men have some type of God-given authority over *all* women. That, in fact, is a heretical notion that has led to serious spiritual and sexual abuse when taken literally.

Christian women who are called and anointed by God to minister in the church do not have to be covered by a man in order to have a legitimate spiritual impact on the lives of people. However, this passage in 1 Corinthians 11 should serve as a warning to all women who aspire to ministry that they should never use their freedom in Christ to dishonor their husbands or anyone else. Jesus does not bless an arrogant attitude. Women who aspire to serve as pastors, teachers, prophets or associate ministers must be held to the same standards of character that all elders are called to emulate in 1 Timothy 3. In fact, when Paul lists the qualifiers for women ministers in 1 Timothy 3:11, his first requirement is that they be "dignified." Part of that dignity is the result of showing respect to their husbands.

3. There is no "gender hierarchy" in the kingdom of God.

Paul's corrective advice to the Corinthians regarding head coverings, particularly his words in 1 Corinthians 11:3 about man's headship over woman ("the man is the head of a woman"), has often been used to establish a form of heirarchy in the church: God rules over men, men rule over women. But is this really the message of Scripture? Does God speak to men, and then ask them to represent Him to women? Of course not!

When the Father chose to enact His plan of redemption, He began the process by visiting an unmarried young woman in Israel named Mary. God did not consult with her father to ask permission or to announce His plans, nor did he appear first to Joseph and ask him to explain the process of the incarnation to his fiancée. In fact, Joseph struggled to understand God's purpose until an angel made it clear to him.

The Bible is full of accounts of women who responded directly to the promptings of the Holy Spirit, apart from the involvement of any man. Hannah, for example, was so burdened with God's desire to bring a deliverer to Israel that she wept in deep spiritual travail until the promise was given of a deliverer. The male spiritual authority in her life, the priest Eli, was so out of touch with God's plan for the nation that he did not understand why Hannah was so burdened or recognize that it was the Spirit of God praying through her when she groaned in intercession in the temple. In Hannah's case, God had to bypass the man to find a woman who would birth His will in prayer. (See 1 Samuel 1:1–28.)

God does not view women on a basement level, as if they are an inferior order of creatures situated "under" the males of the species. He views us all as His children, male and female, and He holds us all accountable for our actions. If a woman sins, God does not seek out the man who is responsible for her misdeed. Also, if she is faithful to the Lord, God does not search for the man responsible for her and then reward him instead.

Yet despite our equality, in marriage God has required a mutuality of love and submission. Paul underscores this when he writes, "However, in the Lord, neither is woman independent of man, nor is man independent of woman" (1 Cor. 11:11). Because he is correcting the Corinthian women for being disrespectful of their husbands, Paul stresses in this passage that wives must display a compliant attitude. He expects wives to be submissive, even as he expects husbands to treat their wives in a loving and respectful manner. Once a man and woman are married, they are *one*. They cannot think independently, as if the other spouse is less important.

An Alternative Translation

This passage about women wearing head coverings in 1 Corinthians 11:2–16 is tricky to interpret, mostly because Paul seems to contradict himself later in 2 Corinthians 3:18 when he exhorts all believers to behold the Lord's glory "with unveiled face." Why does he encourage Christians to worship God without veils in one passage, yet seemingly encourages the use of veils in another?

The answer may be found in a grammatical technicality. Greek scholars of the New Testament have suggested that certain verses in 1 Corinthians 11 may actually be quotes from a letter that was written to Paul by leaders in Corinth. Paul, in fact, refers to these letters in 1 Corinthians 7:1 when he says, "Now concerning the things about which you wrote." His answers to their specific dilemmas form the basis of his epistle.[7]

Lie #5

The Greek language had no punctuation as we do in English to set apart quotations or quoted material. Therefore it is possible that a verse such as 1 Cor. 11:10, "Therefore the woman ought to have a symbol of authority on her head, because of the angels," was a quote from the letter Paul received. The church leaders in Corinth, who came from a Jewish rabbinical tradition, were quoting their rabbinical rules and regulations about head coverings. Yet Paul seems to counter their argument in the next verse, when he says, "However, in the Lord, neither is woman independent of man, nor is man independent of woman" (v. 11).

He contradicts them again in verse 13 by saying, "Judge for yourselves: is it proper for a woman to pray to God with head uncovered?" Then, after explaining that a woman's hair is enough of a covering for her head, he makes this curious statement in verse 16: "But if one is inclined to be contentious, we have no other practice, nor have the churches of God."

The Greek here can actually be translated, "We have no such custom" (see KJV) rather than "We have no other practice." In other words, it is possible that Paul was saying this: "If you want to fight over this, then let me say clearly that the gospel of Christ does not require us to wear veils."

This interpretation certainly makes more sense. Those traditionalists who maintain any other view must then be forced to adopt the strange view that God intends women to wear head coverings during worship in the twenty-first century!

A Woman's True Covering

Of the many women ministers I respect, author and Bible teacher Alice Smith is one of my personal favorites. An ordained Southern Baptist from Houston, Texas, Alice ministers mainly in charismatic circles and has become widely known as an authority on intercession. She is also a skilled practitioner on the subject of deliverance. She prays with authority, and when she casts demons out of people, the spirits come out screaming. But the main reason I respect Alice so much is that her ministry flows out of a deep, intimate relationship with the Lord. In fact, her most popular book, *Beyond the Veil,* is known as a handbook for developing intimacy with God.

The key point of Alice's book is that when Jesus came to redeem us, He paid the ultimate price so that He could bridge the chasm that separated Him from His people. When He spilled His blood at Calvary, God's very presence entered the temple in Jerusalem and tore in half the thick veil that kept us from entering the holy of holies. From that moment on, because of the Savior's obedience, we no longer must linger in the outer courts of the temple. We can come boldly into His presence and enjoy the pleasures of knowing the Father face to face.

Alice Smith enjoys this closeness with God. But the sad truth is that many women in the church today do not believe they can come boldly into the Father's presence because the church has told them they must wait outside the door—simply because of their gender. Some women actually believe that they are disqualified from ever having a close, personal relationship with the Lord because they are women. They have swallowed the despicable lie that says that their husbands must "represent them" in the heavenly throne room. Unmarried and divorced women have struggled with the idea that because they do not have a man in their lives to cover them, they too must live on the outskirts of the Lord's presence.

This is a revolting heresy. Jesus did not shed His blood for men only. When He suffered at Calvary, women were there at the foot of His cross—and those same women bravely identified with His death three days later when they brought spices to His tomb on Easter morning. And when He commissioned them to be witnesses of His resurrection, He did not require them to secure a male "covering" first.

Jesus' blood was shed for all women, and it is the only covering they will ever need. Blood-bought women don't need a man to bring them closer to God. Blood-bought women don't need a man to legitimize their ministries. Blood-bought women don't need a man to "cover" their spiritual endeavors or to replace the leadership of the Holy Spirit in their lives.

The blood of Christ is a woman's true covering. For the church to require anything more is to renounce our faith.

Chapter 5
Questions for Discussion

1. Discuss what happened to Shirley Arnold during her ministry experience in Romania. Have you ever encountered attitudes toward women similar to those that the Romanian church leaders exhibited?

2. Have you ever heard a church leader tell a woman that she could not minister in a particular setting because there was no man to "cover" her? Explain the situation.

3. Read 1 Corinthians 11:1−16 carefully. What do you think Paul means when he says "the man is the head of a woman" in verse 3?

4. Explain why Paul seems to be exhorting the women in Corinth to wear a head covering at church, even though these women know they do not need to be covered in order to be accepted by God.

Women who work in the mission field must be careful to recognize the leadership of man in ordering the affairs of the kingdom of God. We must not allow... the ability and efficiency of so many of our female helpers, nor even the exceptional faculty for leadership and organization which some of them have displayed in their work, to discredit the natural and predestined headship of man in Missions, as well as in the Church of God.[1]

—Directive from a Baptist leader in 1888,
responding to the large number of women
headed to the mission field

When a man is drowning, you don't send a lady out to rescue him. You send a great, big he-man.[2]

American fundamentalist leader Fred Smith,
spokesman of the Men and Religion
Forward Movement of 1912

One reason why women are taking leadership positions is that the man has too often failed to take his place. When men are weak, women must be strong. Men should willingly step forward to lead the church in every area, but often the men are weak and lazy.... Someone has to lead, so the women step in and take control.[3]

—Fundamentalist Baptist leader David W. Cloud,
in a 1998 article in his *O Timothy* magazine

Lie #6

Women who exhibit strong leadership qualities pose a serious danger to the church.

When delegates to the Southern Baptist Convention's annual meeting gathered in 1929, leaders agreed to allow the president of the Women's Missionary Union (WMU) to address their group for the first time. But when she stood to speak, a number of male delegates got up from their chairs and stormed out of the room in protest. They caused such a commotion that the Baptists were forced to hammer out an odd compromise: They decided that the WMU president could speak only if she gave her report in a Sunday school room rather than in the main hall.[4]

The reason for this uproar was that certain male clergy were afraid that by allowing a woman to speak from a pulpit, they would be violating what they called "the dictum of St. Paul"—the apostle Paul's directive in 1 Timothy 2:12 that prohibits women from having "authority over a man." It isn't clear why this poor WMU president was not considered to be exercising as much authority over her male audience when she spoke in a smaller room. In fact, what the Baptists did in this case was irrational. The same can be said for the completely illogical way the church today views the issue of women in spiritual authority.

In a previous chapter we addressed the cultural context of Paul's words in his letter to Timothy, and we noted that his injunction was issued to solve a local problem in the Ephesian church caused by certain uneducated women who were spreading dangerous gnostic doctrines. Yet today, because so many conservative Christians have viewed 1 Timothy 2:12 ("I do not allow a woman to teach or exercise authority over a man") as a universal injunction—to be applied to all churches at all times—we have cultivated a bizarre fear of strong women who preach or teach. This is a strange view indeed, for three reasons:

- First, we know from Scripture that women held the office of prophet under the Old Covenant and that under the New Covenant the apostle Paul himself placed women in positions of authority in the early church, even at a time when females in secular society were barred from pursuing education or leadership roles.

- Second, the Bible challenges *men and women* alike to be strong and courageous in their faith and in their response to the Great Commission. There is no reason to assume that Jesus intended only males to evangelize the world. Both men and women are called to "go" and to "teach." Timidity is never portrayed as a virtue in the Scriptures, for either gender.

- Third, the history of Christianity is full of examples of strong, godly women who achieved remarkable breakthroughs for the kingdom of God. To say that women should not display spiritual strength or do exploits in the name of Jesus is to discredit everything that Christian women have done throughout history to further the gospel.

If we want to stake a claim that women shouldn't lead the church, are we prepared to say that everything women have done to expand the kingdom of God was a mistake? Is the Salvation

Army an illegitimate organization because a strong, vocal woman preacher was a driving force behind it? Do we really want to negate the countless missionary breakthroughs made in the nineteenth and twentieth centuries in China and India, since so many women—such as Amy Carmichael (1867–1951), Bertha Smith (1888–1988) or Marie Monsen (1878–1962)—were responsible for the pioneering work there?

If we look at the history of revival movements, it is clear that whenever there has been a deepening of spiritual passion and holiness in the church and a corresponding call to evangelism, women have responded to the call to ministry even when it was culturally unacceptable for them to do so. This was true during the Second Great Awakening in the United States, which unleashed an army of women to fund missionary movements and to lead the abolitionist cause. It was also obvious in the early days of the Pentecostal revival, which mobilized women preachers to blaze trails in foreign and domestic mission fields. These women, including healing evangelist Lilian Yeomans (1861–1942), Carrie Judd Montgomery (1858–1946), Minnie Draper (1858–1921), Ida Robinson (1891–1946), Aimee Semple McPherson (1890–1944) and Florence Crawford (1872–1936), started churches that still flourish today.[5]

These women were not looking for a spotlight or a pulpit, nor were they out to win an argument or to prove that women are better than men. They were prayer warriors who loved the Word of God and used it skillfully to combat the evils of their day. They were mothers of the faith who nurtured new converts with the milk of salvation and trained their disciples to pursue spiritual maturity. They were brave pioneers who conducted nightly evangelistic campaigns and healing crusades in tents with sawdust floors at a time when Pentecostals were often run out of town by rock-throwing antagonists.

These women were reluctant leaders. They weren't seeking to usurp authority over men, nor did they oppose male leadership. They were not eager to become public speakers; most of them went through a painful process of objection, surrender and consecration before they crucified their timidity and relented to the call of God. Aimee Semple McPherson, who founded the International Church of the Foursquare Gospel in Los Angeles in 1923, described this anguish in her autobiography.

When she heard the Holy Spirit tell her to "Go," Aimee said: "I knew . . . that if I did not go into the work as a soul-winner and get back into the will of God, Jesus would take me to Himself before He would permit me to go on without Him and be lost. Oh, don't you ever tell me that a woman cannot be called to preach the gospel! If any man ever went through one hundredth part of the hell on earth that I lived in, those months when out of God's will and work, they would never say that again. With my remaining strength, I managed to gasp, 'Yes—Lord—I'll—go.' And I did."[6]

Women who have given their lives to serve Jesus on the front lines deserve our respect. But in the American church, we typically have turned our backs on our sisters when they have dared to suggest that God has drafted them into His army. The strongest and most determined of these female warriors learned to endure the ridicule, but we will never know how many women gave up the fight and abandoned the call because the church required them to bury their spiritual gifts.

Adding Insult to Injury

Women in many denominations today have encountered rejection when they stepped out in public ministry. Jill Briscoe, a prominent evangelical author who pastors a church with her husband in Milwaukee, Wisconsin, told *Christianity Today* in 1996 that she was silenced a few years ago when she began to teach the Bible to a group of three thousand teenagers at a youth conference.

"I introduced my subject and opened the Scriptures and read them and began to explain them," Briscoe said. "At that point a pastor stood up and told me, 'Stop! In the name of the Lord!' and said that I was out of order. He then rebuked my husband, saying that he should be ashamed to allow his wife to usurp his authority. He then took his young people out, and several other people followed."[7]

In some charismatic and Pentecostal circles, the label "Jezebel" is often pinned on women who have teaching or leadership skills or who are bold enough to express their opinions to their pastors. The insulting implication is that any Christian woman who steps outside the lines of ecclesiastical propriety and presumes to speak for God or displays any level of courage is labeled rebellious or conniving.

In some cases, godly women have been accused of being witches because they broke with religious tradition and stood in a pulpit. I witnessed this sick attitude with my own eyes a few years ago while I was attending a prayer conference with several thousand charismatic Christians in Colorado. When my friend Cindy Jacobs, an internationally known Bible teacher and prayer mobilizer, was introduced as the keynote speaker, two ministers who were sitting in front of me turned to each other and began to pray quietly as Cindy approached the podium. The men had no idea that I could hear them.

These men were prominent leaders I respected, but I was shocked when I heard their whispers. "Lord, we bind the power of the devil from bewitching this audience," one of the men said, adding, "We bind the power of Jezebel in the name of Jesus." These men obviously believed that because Cindy was a woman, the crowd would automatically come under a spirit of deception when she taught them. They didn't have the gall to challenge Cindy openly, but they felt it necessary to ask God to neutralize the negative impact they believed would result when a female taught the Bible to an audience that included a large number of men.

Pinning the Jezebel label on a woman of God is a blatant attempt at character assassination. After all, Jezebel was the personification of evil. We read in 1 Kings 18–19 that she wielded tyrannical power over Israel through her spiritual ties to the cult of Baal. From her position as queen, sitting beside King Ahab, Jezebel was responsible for the murder of many of Israel's true prophets. Her strategy was to intimidate the righteous followers of God while promoting Baal worship—so that the sexual perversion associated with her brand of paganism would eventually control the entire country.

This queen was eventually overthrown, along with her wicked husband, but she is mentioned again in the New Testament as a metaphor for sexual immorality and occult deception. In the apostle John's message to the church in Thyatira (Rev. 2:20), he issues a warning from Christ about "the woman Jezebel" who "calls herself a prophetess, and she teaches and leads My bond-servants astray, so that they commit acts of immorality and eat things sacrificed to idols."

Jezebel was most likely not this woman's real name. John used a form of code language in the Book of Revelation to protect the vulnerable churches from persecution. He pinned the name Jezebel on this self-appointed female church leader in Thyatira because she was claiming to speak for God and yet was promoting sexual sin and idolatrous worship. She represents the ultimate false prophet, and it is insidious to compare her to godly Christian women who are teaching and preaching the truth of the gospel.

It is offensive to suggest that a woman who loves Jesus Christ, walks in personal holiness and upholds the Word of God with integrity is influenced by a "spirit of Jezebel"—just because she is female! Yet I have lost count of the number of women who have told me that they were accused of being a "Jezebel influence" because they functioned as a pastor, an evangelist or even a lay leader.

Julie Nelson,* who at one time co-pastored a church with her husband, Mike,* in Tampa, told me that she struggled for years in her denomination because women who held positions in public ministry were viewed with suspicion by most male pastors. Julie was often shunned, and her husband was told that he had a spiritual problem because his wife "was not in total submission" to him. "The men in our group were considered weak and 'not in charge' if their wife had a ministry," she said.

After many years of ministry together, a leader in their denomination told Julie's husband that he should stop sharing his most intimate concerns and dreams with her. This unusual brand of marriage counseling was designed to keep him in a position of dominance—by forcing his wife to be less involved in his life!

"The counselor was basically accusing me of being a Jezebel," Julie said. "Mike heeded his counsel, and it almost led to the destruction of our marriage. But we were able to regroup; we began to communicate again, and we eventually moved on to a new church where I was allowed to function in my ministry gifts."

*Names have been changed to protect privacy.

Lie #6

Silly Superstitions

Five hundred years ago, Protestant reformer John Knox taught that God brings a curse on a nation if it is governed by a woman. Never mind the fact that most nations in that period were led by wicked kings who did not honor the law of God or abide by any rule of Christian integrity. Yet Knox believed the moral condition of a nation would abruptly deteriorate if a queen took the throne.

In a tract he wrote in 1558 titled "The First Blast Against the Monstrous Regiment of Women," the Scottish reformer wrote: "If women take upon them the office which God hath assigned to men, they shall not escape the divine malediction."[8] Although he directed most of his attack toward two Roman Catholic queens, Mary Tudor of England and Mary Guise of Scotland, and he referred to them both as "Jezebels," Knox made it clear that he believed God always opposes women who hold positions of authority.

That same view still lingers in the modern church. In the early 1980s, when so many religious conservatives were active in the political arena in the United States, some of them opposed President Ronald Reagan's appointment of Judge Sandra Day O'Connor to the Supreme Court. Their fundamentalist views of male headship in society did not allow for a woman to assume a top position in civil authority.

Justice O'Connor did not lead to our nation to ruin, any more than Margaret Thatcher's eleven-year term as Prime Minister triggered the downfall of Great Britain. In fact, in the mid-1990s, some of the most vocal women elected to the U.S. Congress were Bible-believing, evangelical Christians who stood bravely against the status quo by challenging legalized abortion, the tobacco industry and foreign aid to countries that tolerate religious persecution.

Our society has become more accepting of women in roles of authority in the secular realm. Yet Christians continue to reject women who have the spiritual gifts necessary to provide pastoral leadership, administrative ability or prophetic insight to our churches and denominations. Clergy in some groups have been afraid even to allow lay women to lead church committees or serve on church boards.

In many churches in the United States, Christian men have developed a superstitious notion that if they listen to a woman preach, attend a Sunday school class taught by a woman or allow a woman to provide any form of spiritual counseling to them directly, they are violating an unwritten law that forbids women from occupying a place of authority in their lives. They also fear that if they do this, they will come under some type of spell that leaves them deceived and spiritually weakened.

I know some men who will not watch a television broadcast or a videotape of a sermon by someone like charismatic Bible teacher Joyce Meyer because they feel that to listen to her would rob them of their spiritual authority as men. Some men will not read a book by a female Christian author! And some evangelical pastors advise the men in their church never to receive spiritual counsel from a woman, even their wives, since doing so violates the mistaken notion that God intended only men to preach to men.

This behavior is rooted in a fear that if a man submits to a woman by listening to her counsel, his own maleness will be diminished. How foolish! If the Bible is our guide and not cultural bias, then we need to consider the many times in Scripture in which women influenced men or exercised godly authority over them. We also need to see that there are instances in Scripture when men affirmed and honored the spiritual leadership of women.

Judges 4 tells us that at one time in history a woman held the highest position of spiritual authority in Israel. Conservative Bible scholars have struggled with this passage, and some go so far as to teach that Deborah's leadership was not God-appointed at all. They quote Judges 17:6, which says that the inhabitants of Israel "did what was right in [their] own eyes," and then maintain that this climate of disobedience resulted in a "curse" of female leadership. That argument doesn't make sense, however, because Judges 17:6 applies to a time period after Deborah's reign.

The Bible clearly states that God anointed Deborah as judge over Israel, gave her wisdom and prophetic counsel, and granted a forty-year period of peace as a result of her effective leadership.

(See Judges 4:1–5; 5:31.) And the men who honored her authority were blessed.

We read in Judges 4:8 that Barak, Israel's chief military commander, refused to go into battle without Deborah after she unveiled the Lord's strategy to defeat the Canaanites. It was not an admission of fear on Barak's part when he asked Deborah to accompany him into the fray. He was not a "mama's boy" who felt unsure about his masculinity. On the contrary, Barak recognized that Deborah was an anointed servant of God and that the mantle of heaven's authority rested on her. Because she had the plan of victory, he wanted to stay close to her. He simply refused to fight without the Lord's prophet by his side.

In today's church, we need an army of Baraks who are so desperate to hear the word of the Lord that they are willing to humble themselves and receive it from whomever God chooses to speak through—even if that prophet is a woman. We as men need to swallow our male pride and our haughty "I know better than you, dear" attitudes. If we are truly walking in spiritual brokenness, we will not care whether the Holy Spirit speaks through a man, a woman, a child or a donkey. We will simply want God, and we will place no stock in the imperfect clay vessel God chooses.

Where Are the Priscillas?

In Acts 18:24–28, we read that a skilled preacher named Apollos, a zealous convert from Judaism, was teaching the message of Jesus in Ephesus. But because he had never been instructed properly about water baptism or the infilling of the Holy Spirit, Paul's co-workers, Priscilla and Aquila, "took him aside and explained to him the way of God more accurately" (v. 26).

Was Apollos spiritually emasculated when he submitted to Priscilla's correction? Absolutely not. His ministry was strengthened because of the helpful input he received from this wise disciple, who most likely functioned in an apostolic role as a teacher and church planter. She is commended by Paul as one of his "fellow workers" in Romans 16:3. And in 1 Corinthians 16:16, the apostle urges his followers to submit to "everyone who helps in the work and labors." Since "everyone" in this passage obviously includes Priscilla as well as Junia, Phoebe and the other women who assisted Paul on his apostolic team, we can clearly see that he asked the early church to acknowledge the authority of the women who worked with him.

Apollos most likely felt indebted to Priscilla and her husband for their mentorship. She became a mother in the faith to him. What would have happened in the New Testament church if Apollos had been too proud to receive correction and theological instruction from her? It's possible he would have fallen into serious error, thereby thwarting the work of God in Asia Minor and perhaps even derailing his ministry. What similar pitfalls could be avoided in our day if more men were willing to receive counsel, correction and insight from seasoned women ministers?

There are numerous other examples in the Scriptures of godly women who provided counsel, instruction or correction to men. The prophetess Huldah was sought out by King Josiah's top leaders for her advice about the spiritual condition of their nation (2 Kings 22:14–20). When the elderly prophetess Anna recognized that the baby Jesus was the long-awaited Messiah, she proclaimed His identity to His parents and to all who came into the temple. She was, in fact, one of the first people on planet earth to publicly proclaim the gospel of the New Covenant. And the apostle Paul mentions a total of seven women when listing his trusted co-laborers; these were women who functioned as pastors, evangelists, deacons or apostles.

It seems odd that Christian men would have difficulty accepting the authority of women when every man has had to submit to the instruction and discipline of his own mother. In the Christian family we expect a mother to exercise authority: She not only provides nurturing love and sustenance to her children but also brings swift discipline when necessary, and her children benefit most when her instruction is rigorous. Don't we need the same qualities in our spiritual mothers? Shouldn't we expect them to rule with godly authority?

In African American churches in the United States there has been a long-cherished tradition of acknowledging "church mothers." These are usually the wisest, most mature women, those who have walked with God for many years and who are viewed as saintly models of virtue and spirituality. Although their primary role is to teach the younger women, these matriarchs often have broad authority to speak to the entire congregation—and when they speak it is with the authority of a mother. They are always seated in the front of the church. When one of them has a word of reproof to offer, it can sting. When one of them has an exhortation, the attitude of most people in the room is, "Look out, Mother has a word from God."

Most Christian men, whether they admit it or not, would not be where they are today had it not been for the Priscillas and other spiritual mothers who came alongside them at the right time and gave a timely word of encouragement or counsel. Because of insecurity, we think our masculinity is deficient if we admit we need the insights that these women provide. The church as a whole would be better off if we would ask God to shatter our male pride so we can make room for these women to function in their divine giftings.

Strength Is Her Clothing

Nowhere in the Bible are women called to be weak. A careful study of women in Scripture reveals that the godly women who served His purpose in their generation displayed courage, endured hardship and exercised the kind of faith that overcomes impossible odds. Righteous women in the Bible did not sit in the back of the church with their mouths shut or wait until they got permission to challenge injustice.

The great women of the Bible were fearless. Remember the Jewish midwives, who put their own lives in jeopardy in Egypt to protect the infants who had been sentenced to death by Pharaoh. Remember Rahab, who disobeyed the authorities in Jericho because she knew God was with the Israelite spies. Her faith saved her household and placed her in the lineage of Christ.

Remember Deborah in Judges 4, who led her nation into a forty-year period of peace because she sought the Lord's battle strategy and believed He was able to overthrow an army that outnumbered Israel's. Remember Jael, whose bravery led her to drive a tent peg through the head of Sisera—thus ending the war with the

Canaanites. Remember Esther, who placed her own life on the line because she believed God could use her to turn the heart of a king and save thousands of lives.

If we examine the "model woman" described in Proverbs 31, it's obvious that she is not a mousy housewife or a timid wall-flower. She did not allow patriarchal society to define her worth in terms of her sexuality, her appearance or her mundane domestic duties. We are told that she "girds herself with strength, and strengthens her arms" (v. 17, NKJV). This doesn't mean she was a female body-builder; the passage refers to her strength of character and her readiness for spiritual battle.

She was prepared for a fight if the enemy attacked, and the fact that "her lamp does not go out by night" (v. 18, NKJV) infers that she is also a woman of persevering prayer. Genuine spiritual mothers are watchful. They keep a vigilant eye on the church, ready to launch countermeasures when they see danger approaching. Notice also that "strength and dignity are her clothing" (v. 25). She does not allow her self-image to be created for her by the media or by what religious protocol demands or by what men say she can or can't do. She puts on strength and dignity. She knows who she is in Christ. Her identity is in Him. Although she recognizes her limitations in the natural realm, she knows that the Spirit of God dwells in her. She confidently declares, "I can do all things through Christ who strengthens me" (Phil. 4:13, NKJV).

A major misconception in the church today is that women were created to be weak and shy and that it is abnormal or even perverse for a woman to display qualities of strength. Most often this lie is based on an erroneous interpretation of 1 Peter 3:7, which refers to women as "the weaker vessel" (KJV). In the New American Standard Bible, the passage says:

> You husbands likewise, live with your wives in an under-standing way, *as with a weaker vessel,* since she is a woman; and grant her honor as a fellow heir of the grace of life, so that your prayers may not be hindered.
>
> —EMPHASIS ADDED

Notice that this passage does not directly say that women are weaker. Rather, it exhorts husbands to treat their wives with consideration and respect "as if" their wives were weaker. Peter was most likely not talking about the physical realm. He was not referring to the fact that women are more prone to osteoporosis or breast cancer or that they experience discomfort and hormonal problems during their monthly menstrual cycles. He is simply acknowledging that because of the curse of sin, women are at a disadvantage and need to be protected. He is not putting them down or relegating them to inferior status.

But let's remember that even if women are weaker vessels in one sense, this state has absolutely nothing to do with their fitness for spiritual ministry. After all, what is important for a person in ministry is that the anointing of God is flowing through the vessel—*whether it is weak or strong.* A man who is strong in the natural sense of the word but who has no anointing from God will not accomplish anything of lasting benefit for the kingdom. A woman who is weak in the natural but who moves in the power of the Holy Spirit can change nations.

Rather than argue about whether women are weak, can't we acknowledge that we are all just clay vessels? Whether male or female, we are frail in our humanity and in our tendency to sin. None of us who aspire to the ministry can ever hope to see lives changed by Christ's presence if we rely on our own fleshly abilities. We are called to glory in our weakness so that He might be strong in us.

It's time for the weaker vessels to come forth. Christian women who have lived in the shadows of insignificance need to arise and put on strength. This is the hour that Joel foretold, a time for both the sons and the daughters to prophesy. Women of God, arise! You can't be silent anymore.

Chapter 6
Questions for Discussion

1. Why is it so unfair to compare the evil Jezebel with a Christian woman who aspires to a position of leadership in the church?

2. Give three reasons why we can't universally apply 1 Timothy 2:12 ("I do not allow a woman to teach or exercise authority over a man") to all churches in all time periods.

3. Describe how Barak responded to the leadership of Deborah. How should we apply this today in the church?

4. Why is it significant that Priscilla was involved in bringing theological correction to Apollos' ministry?

5. Read Proverbs 31:10–31 and list the qualities you admire in this virtuous woman. Which qualities indicate that she was a strong person?

6. What do you think the apostle Peter meant when he described women as "weaker vessels" in 1 Peter 3:7?

*Do you not know that you are [each] an Eve? The sentence of
God on this sex of yours lives in this age; the guilt must of
necessity live too. You are the Devil's gateway: You are the
unsealer of that [forbidden] tree: you are the first deserter of
the divine law: you are she who persuaded him whom the devil
was not valiant enough to attack. On account of your desert—
that is, death—even the Son of God had to die.[1]*

—TERTULLIAN (A.D. 155–220)

---

*Woman was evil from the beginnings, a gate of death, a
disciple of the servant, the devil's accomplice, a fount of
deception, a dogstart to godly labours, rust corrupting the
saints; whose perilous face hath overgrown such as had already
become almost angels. Lo, woman is the head of sin, a weapon
of the devil, expulsion from Paradise, mother of guilt,
corruption of the ancient law.[2]*

—FROM A COLLECTION OF VIEWS ON WOMEN COMPILED BY
SALIMBENE, A THIRTEENTH-CENTURY FRANCISCAN MONK (1221–1288)

---

*[A woman] is more carnal than a man, as is clear from her
many carnal abominations. And it should be noted that there
was a defect in the formation of the first woman, since she was
formed from a bent rib, that is, a rib of the breast, which is bent
as it were in contrary direction of a man. And since through this
defect she is an imperfect animal, she always deceives.... Since
[women] are feebler both in mind and body, it is not surprising
that they should come under the spell of witchcraft.[3]*

—DOMINICAN INQUISITORS HEINRICH KRAMER AND JAMES SPRENGER
IN A 1486 TRACT IN WHICH THEY ARGUED THAT WOMEN ARE
THE SOURCE OF ALL WITCHCRAFT

---

*No wickedness comes anywhere near the wickedness of a
woman… Sin began with a woman and thanks to her all must die.*

—FROM THE APOCRYPHA, ECCLESIASTICUS 25:19, 24

Lie #7
Women are more easily deceived than men.

One of the most tragic moments in American religious history occurred in the spring of 1638 when the strict Puritan fathers of Boston excommunicated a devout Christian woman named Anne Hutchinson. Labeled as a dangerous heretic by the leaders of the Massachusetts Bay Colony, Anne was banished and forced to move with her husband and fifteen children to Rhode Island—and later, following his death, to unsettled Long Island. When she and some of her children were killed by Indians in 1643, the men who had overseen her trial told her sympathizers that her death was a clear sign of God's judgment on her for spreading "the vilest errors."[4]

One Calvinist minister, Rev. Thomas Weld, reasoned that since Indians didn't normally stage massacres on Long Island, Hutchinson's violent death must have been God's way of teaching her a lesson. The murder, he said, spared New England from this "woeful woman." Before her banishment, when she was under house arrest in Boston, Weld also spread a rumor that Hutchinson had given birth to thirty monsters during a painful miscarriage.

Thus she eventually came to be known by her Puritan critics as "the American Jezebel"—an evil witch who could not be tolerated.[5]

What was Anne Hutchinson's horrible crime? What heresy did this pious Quaker woman teach that provoked her elders to banish her from the colony? The charges against her seem silly to us in the twenty-first century. She was summoned to court because she dared to hold a women's meeting in her home—a quiet gathering that sometimes attracted up to sixty females, along with a few men who admittedly enjoyed her lectures. (The typical crowd was probably no more than twelve, some historians insist.)

During her talks, she dared to criticize the Sunday sermons of leading Puritan ministers in Boston, and she accused them of preaching a doctrine of works rather than a message of Christ's free grace. A believer in the Holy Spirit's work in every Christian, she also claimed to hear messages directly from God, and she encouraged others to seek their own personal revelations from the Scriptures rather than relying solely on what the pastor spoon-fed his congregation.

Historians Ruth Tucker and Walter Liefeld write that "almost immediately these gatherings were seen as a threat to male authority" in the colony. The church fathers told Hutchinson that her behavior was "not fitting for your sex," and they charged that she wanted to be more "a husband than a wife, a preacher than a hearer, and a magistrate than a subject."[6]

Fearful that her free-thinking, insubordinate attitude would spread like a cancer to other towns in the colony, the Puritans moved swiftly to recommend excommunication. They could not hold tight religious control of Massachusetts if this renegade woman continued promoting her dissenting theological views. So they got rid of her.

There has been some disagreement over whether Anne Hutchinson was banished simply because she was a woman, or because she dared to question the iron-clad Calvinist rules of her day, or both. Some have made her out to be a feminist martyr, bravely dying in the wilderness for the sake of women's rights. But others point out that since many women in Boston supported the cruel judgment against her, the dispute was really more about theology than gender. Regardless of the motives of her accusers, there is no question that Hutchinson was at a disadvantage, since it was extremely unusual in seventeenth-century America for a female to lead a religious meeting—even in her home with only women in attendance. She broke a fundamental rule of colonial Christianity, and she paid dearly for it.

What was at work during Hutchinson's trial, to be sure, was a prevailing attitude that the Puritan fathers had inherited from their chauvinistic forebears. It was the idea that women, by nature, are deceivers—and that they are prone to witchcraft and heresy. The preposterous accusation that Hutchinson had given birth to monsters was in line with the seventeenth-century notion that devils are regularly hatched from the wombs of females. It was the same attitude that later led to the infamous Salem witchcraft trials of 1692, when several Bible-believing Christian women were hanged after being falsely accused of practicing witchcraft.[7]

Sadly, this same attitude motivates modern church leaders to keep women out of positions of spiritual influence. Although evangelicals teach that Jesus Christ paid the full price to redeem men and women from the consequences of original sin, we rarely apply His redemptive grace equally to females. Instead, we've implied that men can be forgiven for Adam's role in the fall of mankind while women must continue to be punished for Eve's sin.

The typical line of reasoning goes like this: Because Eve was deceived in the Garden of Eden, and because her sin preceded Adam's, women are therefore more prone to deception and must be guarded carefully lest they devise some strange teaching and lead God's people astray. Because of a woman's innate gullibility, she must never teach in the church or be allowed to assume spiritual responsibility of any kind. Some Christians, in fact, believe that if a woman is allowed to teach, she will automatically set in motion a process of deception that will end in disaster. This is not a biblical concept, but it has been promoted for centuries by the church.

It is still taught today. David Cloud, a Christian author and minister based in Oak Harbor, Washington, preaches this position in numerous articles distributed by the Fundamentalist Baptist News Service. He wrote in the year 2000:

The woman has a different makeup than the man. She was designed for a different role in life—that of a wife and mother. Her emotional, psychological, and rational makeup are geared perfectly for this, but she was not designed for leadership. In the Garden of Eden the devil deceived her. This was not true for Adam. He sinned, but he was not deceived. Eve had allowed herself to be thrust into a position of decision-making she was not supposed to occupy. It is no coincidence that women have been responsible for starting many of the false Christian movements and have played key roles in spiritism, New Age, mind science cults and such. Human nature has not changed, and neither have God's restrictions against women preachers.[8]

Going on a Witch Hunt

This view of woman as inherently evil and more easily deceived was not a new idea to the early church fathers. It was a pagan idea inherited from ancient Greek culture, best exemplified by the mythical story of Pandora. Out of curiosity, Pandora opened a box that she had been told to keep shut, and out of it came every vile demon of poverty, war, disease, ignorance and misfortune. Woman, therefore, was the official scapegoat; she became the source of all evil in the world. The most revered Greek philosophers believed this, and they taught that women are inferior, ignorant and prone to deception as well as to sexual infidelity. Plato, in fact, taught that women are a lower form of life and that men who do not live honorably will be reincarnated as women in another life.

Jews in the second and third centuries also promoted the view that women are the source of evil. In fact, rabbis during that period were known to recite a prayer thanking God that they were not women: "Praised be God that He has not created me a gentile; praised be God that He has not created me a woman; praised be God that He has not created me an ignorant man."[9] One popular Jewish proverb of that period described woman as "a pitcher full of filth."[10]

Theologians Richard and Catherine Clark Kroeger note that Jewish tradition in the early centuries after the coming of Christ required that women walk in front of corpses at funerals because Eve was responsible for bringing death into the world. They write: "Menstruation, labor pains, and subjugation were considered consequences of [Eve's] primary role in the fall.... [Jewish women] must light the Sabbath lamps because Eve had brought darkness. In further recompense, they must prepare the dough offering because Adam, the pure dough of the world, had been corrupted by his spouse. These requirements served as constant reminders that women still bore the stigma of Eve's sin."[11]

This degrading view of women entered into the early church. Early Christian theologians such as Tertullian called woman "the devil's gateway," suggesting that because Eve led Adam astray, women must forever pay for her sin by living in absolute subjection to their male masters—who are more spiritually enlightened. John Chrysostom (circa A.D. 400) taught that Eve "ruined all." Some church fathers at that time began to teach that Adam was completely innocent in the encounter with Satan in the Garden of Eden and that Eve was fully responsible for the Fall.

This "blame Eve for everything" philosophy led to some bizarre teachings in the early church that impacted medieval Christianity for centuries. Some church leaders suggested that Adam's temptation in the Garden was the result of seeing Eve's nakedness; they believed that the fundamental cause of sin in the world was the lure of female sexuality. Her beauty, therefore, became her curse. Sexual attractiveness was viewed as a satanic plot to pull men into a web of feminine deceit.

Because the church had demonized a woman's God-given sexuality, celibacy was viewed as superior to marriage, and men who abstained from sex with women were considered spiritually pure because they had not been tainted by female carnality. At the same time, women were told that the only true path to holiness was to deny their sexuality and remain perpetual virgins. St. Augustine, in fact, believed that only men were made in the image of God and that the only way women could please the Lord was to deny sex and marriage altogether.

Thomas Aquinas, the medieval theologian, taught that women were "defective and misbegotten," and he too believed that Eve's body was the cause of Adam's sin. Aquinas also promoted the idea that the serpent approached Eve rather than Adam because she was more vulnerable to deception.[12] This was echoed a few centuries later by Heinrich Kramer and James Sprenger, two Catholic theologians, who argued during the period of the Inquisition in 1486 that women are more likely to become witches because females were created by God with serious defects.

They wrote: "Women are naturally more impressionable... Since they are feebler in mind and body, it is not surprising that they should come under the spell of witchcraft." In one chapter of their book, *Witch's Hammer,* the authors suggested that women often willingly submit to sexual intercourse with demons and that this devilish ritual was the source of much of the evil in the world.[13]

The Inquisition period had been launched in 1320 when Pope John XXII formalized the persecution of witchcraft. For the next four hundred years, women were subjected to unspeakable horrors at the hands of the church—all in the name of Christ—in order to rid Europe of sorcery. Those who were accused of witchcraft (in most cases unjustly) were taken to the torture chamber or the gallows. Some were stripped and shaved because their inquisitors believed they bore hidden markings on their bodies that proved they belonged to the devil. Some had needles inserted into their eyes; many had their tongues pulled out.

These witch hunts were particularly cruel in Germany, France, Switzerland, Poland and Scotland. In her book *The Dark Side of Christian History,* Helen Ellerbe notes that accused witches were often subjected to sexual mutilation. Their breasts and genitals were sometimes maimed with pincers, pliers and hot irons. If the women did not confess their involvement in sorcery, they were usually taken to the stake and burned—sometimes while their children watched.[14]

Ellerbe points out that these women were rarely given a fair trail—if any type of hearing at all—and evidence was provided by dubious witnesses. In many cases these supposed witches were killed by angry mobs, in the same way that black men were lynched in the early 1900s in the United States because someone falsely accused them of rape. Medieval women often were blamed for misfortunes that happened just because they walked by or were seen near the scene of a crime. One Scottish woman, for example, was accused of witchcraft and burned at the stake because someone saw her petting a cat at the same time a batch of beer went sour!

Ellerbe writes: "In England, where there were no inquisitional courts and where witch-hunting offered little or no financial award, many women were killed for witchcraft by mobs. Instead of following any judicial procedure, these mobs used methods to ascertain guilt of witchcraft such as 'swimming a witch,' where a woman would be bound and thrown into water to see if she floated. The water, as the medium of baptism, would either reject her and prove her guilty of witchcraft, or the woman would sink and be proven innocent, albeit dead from drowning."[15]

No one knows today how many innocent women died during the horrors of the Inquisition. Many secular feminists today consider it on the same level as the Nazi Holocaust—but this cannot be proven because death records are scant. One bishop in Germany claimed to have killed nineteen hundred witches in five years. A Lutheran leader, Benedict Carpzov, claimed to have sentenced twenty thousand devil worshipers to death—most of them female. One historical account suggests that the female population of two French villages—all except two women—was wiped out in 1586.[16]

What motivated church leaders to launch such a vicious attack on women? Those who had any knowledge of the Bible were known to quote an Old Testament passage, Exodus 22:18, in which God told Israel: "Thou shalt not suffer a witch to live" (KJV). But generally, medieval clerics simply believed that women were evil by nature and more prone to superstition and devilish activity; that is why so many women who were falsely accused had no chance of proving their innocence. Church leaders had decided they were guilty from birth. And as a result of this prejudice, thousands of women—perhaps even more—lost their lives.

Who Were the Greatest Deceivers?

Are women more prone to witchcraft and deception? Although women have threatened the church with false teachings, history proves that men have been more involved in spreading Satan's lies.

Almost every false religion on earth today, in fact, was founded by a man—including Islam, Buddhism and atheistic communism. Most of the world's pseudo-Christian cults, such as Sun Myung Moon's Unification Church, were started by men. Each of the men listed below spun webs of deception that have trapped millions:

- **Allan Kardec** (1804–1869), a French educator, founded the modern spiritist movement. He believed that spirits from the invisible realm seek to communicate with those in the material world, and he invited millions to investigate the paranormal through books such as *The Guide for Mediums and Invocators.* Kardec's writings are especially popular in Latin America; in fact, spiritism in Brazil is often referred to as *kardecismo* because of his influence.[17]

- **Joseph Smith** (1805–1844) founded what became the Mormon church after he claimed to have been visited by God and Jesus Christ while he was praying on a hilltop in upstate New York. He later claimed that an angel showed him where to find a mysterious set of golden plates, written in what he called "reformed Egyptian." These writings, which Smith claims he translated with supernatural spectacles provided by the angel, became the *Book of Mormon*—now the basis for a religion that claims eleven million adherents around the world. His claims and his bogus "translation" have been proven to be a hoax.[18]

- **Allister Crowley** (1875–1947) was raised in a Plymouth Brethren home in England, but he later rejected Christianity and pioneered an occult religion known as Thelema. He believed Christianity was "the curse of the world," and he shared his occult beliefs through books including *Magick in Theory and Practice* and *Tarot Divination.* An admitted bisexual, he challenged his followers to throw off sexual restraints in order to discover the occult world.[19]

- **Gerald B. Gardner** (1884–1964) is known today as the father of modern witchcraft. He was initiated into a coven in 1939 in England and began to explore what he called "the Stone Age origins of witchcraft." The first avowed witch to write books about the occult, Gardner authored *Fellowship of the Crotona* and *Hermetic Order of the Golden Dawn*—books that are read widely today by the estimated five hundred thousand Wiccans who practice some form of neo-pagan nature worship in the United States.[20]

- **Edgar Cayce** (1877–1945) claimed that he had tapped into a "higher consciousness" and then taught his followers how to do psychic readings. Although he did not have more than a sixth grade education, millions read his books and believed his bizarre prophecies—which included predictions about the emergence of the lost continent of Atlantis. Today his followers operate a school of psychic science in Virginia.[21]

- **L. Ron Hubbard** (1911–1986) founded the Church of Scientology, which has lured thousands of people into adopting a bizarre view of mental and spiritual energy. Hubbard claimed that he learned secrets of mental health from his childhood encounters with Blackfoot Indians and Chinese magicians. Later in life, he claimed to have had a spiritual experience in an ancient burial ground in Guam. His 1950 best-selling book, *Dianetics: The Science of Mental Health,* was rejected by health professionals, but it became the cornerstone of his new religion—which gained popularity in the late twentieth century after several American film stars became Scientologists.[22]

The list of men who invented other deceptive doctrines could fill entire books. What about Charles Taze Russell, the founder of the Jehovah's Witnesses? Or Mirza Ali Muhammad, the Iranian businessman who found the Baha'i faith? Or Harvey Spencer, who established the Ancient Mystical Order of the Rosae Crucis, more commonly known as the Rosicrucians? And what about the devilish, anti-Christian philosophies that were brought into this world through men like Karl Marx, Mao Tse Tung, Freidrich Neitze and Charles Darwin? It's obvious that men throughout the centuries have corrupted millions of minds with lies and spiritual darkness.

This is not to say that women cannot be deceived or that they cannot invent deceptive philosophies. Men and women share a sinful human nature, and they are both prone to evil. But in American history, only three major cultic organizations were founded by women: The Theosophy Society, started in New York by Russian mystic Helena Blavatsky in 1875; the Unity movement, founded by Myrtle Fillmore around 1891; and the Christian Science movement, established by Mary Baker Eddy in the late 1800s. (It must be noted, however, that Eddy's organization could not have been founded without the help of Phineas Parkhurst Quimby, a quack mental healer who used terms such as "the science of Christ" and "the science of man" long before Eddy borrowed the terms from him.)[23]

History proves that men have produced most of the world's cults, false religions and occult movements. Yet women have been unfairly stereotyped as deceivers, and the church is primarily responsible for this degrading form of judgment. Millions of women around the world consider the Christian church a hostile place to turn for spiritual help. Our generation must repent for the mistakes of the past if we expect to reconcile this tension between the genders.

Can We Blame Eve for Everything?

Evangelicals today who still forbid women to enter public ministry almost always do so on the basis of Paul's words in 1 Timothy 2:12, "I do not allow a woman to teach or exercise authority over a man." But they also cite verses 13 and 14 to support the notion that women are barred from teaching or preaching the gospel because they are more easily deceived than men. This passage says:

> For it was Adam who was first created, and then Eve. And it was not Adam who was deceived, but the woman being quite deceived, fell into transgression.

What is Paul saying here? We cannot read these verses out of context. If we examine the situation in Ephesus more carefully, taking into consideration the unique theological problems that plagued the New Testament church, we will discover that Paul cited the creation account in this passage not to place extra blame on Eve but to refute a bizarre teaching that was circulating in Asia Minor at that time.

In the first century, gnostic heretics were mixing Christianity with paganism in a culture that worshiped the female deity known as Artemis, also known as Diana. Often, the gnostics turned Bible stories upside down to distort their meaning. One of their fables stated that Eve actually liberated the world when she disobeyed God. Gnostic heretics (who had both male and female followers) believed that Eve was the "illuminator," and they taught that she brought spiritual liberation to creation when she listened to the serpent. These cultists even believed that after Eve was "enlightened" by eating the forbidden fruit, she became Adam's mother rather than his wife, and they taught that she should be viewed as the progenitor of all mankind. This was a serious form of heresy that challenged the very core of early Christianity.[24]

The gnostics, who traced their origin to Jewish mysticism, had a tradition of twisting the Old Testament. They mixed mythology with the Scriptures, and in the process invented an entirely new religion based on "secret" *gnosis,* or knowledge. Not only did they make Eve a salvation figure, but they taught that Cain was a hero and that Moses was a liar. They also believed that the God of the Old Testament was evil and that the serpent was to be worshiped. That is why gnostics revered snakes and incorporated the worship of serpents in many of their mystical ceremonies.[25]

It was this strange brand of heresy that Paul commissioned Timothy to combat vigorously in the Ephesian church when he said, "Instruct certain men not to teach *strange doctrines*" (1 Tim. 1:3, emphasis added). Paul also warned in 1 Timothy 4:1: "In later times some will fall away from the faith, paying attention to *deceitful spirits and doctrines of demons*" (emphasis added). He also instructed Timothy to avoid "worldly *fables* fit only for old women" (4:7, emphasis added), indicating that older women were involved in spreading these gnostic heresies in Ephesus.[26]

There is no question that Paul was concerned about the threat of mystery religions like gnosticism, and historical evidence proves that these cultic groups were operating in Ephesus at the time he wrote his letter to Timothy. He would have been extremely concerned if the teachings of gnostic priests were infiltrating the church and luring Christian converts away to visit pagan temples. His reference to "old women" may actually be pointing to priestesses who worshiped an "Eve" goddess.

There is ample historical evidence to prove that at the time Paul's first epistle was written to Timothy, a blasphemous cult had developed in or near Ephesus that taught that Eve was really the "Great Mother"—an incarnation of the goddess. They also associated Adam with the goddess' lover, Attis, and taught that he received the gift of life from her. In addition, the gnostics who worshiped Eve also revered the snake, and they believed that she and the serpent shared a mystical union.[24]

How was Paul to respond when he discovered that this bizarre form of blasphemy was actually being taught to some of the converts in Ephesus? If this teaching were tolerated, it would destroy the work he had established in Asia Minor. He had to condemn it. So he spelled out the creation story in no uncertain terms in 1 Timothy 2:13–14 to set the record straight. He wrote:

- *"It was Adam who was first created"* (v. 13). In other words, Eve was not created first, nor was she a "goddess mother." The gnostic idea that she gave life to Adam is a myth.

- *"It was not Adam who was deceived"* (v. 14). Some gnostics believed that Adam was the "bad guy" in the story because he didn't want to join Eve at first when she listened to the serpent. But Paul dispelled this notion.

- *"But the woman being quite deceived, fell into transgression"* (v. 14). Paul made it clear here that Eve was not "enlightened" when she listened to the devil. She made a sinful choice.

It is likely that women were involved in spreading these dangerous doctrines in Ephesus, a city that was dominated by the cult worship of the goddess. The cult promoted ritual prostitu-tion, and its followers believed that spiritual revelations could be obtained through sexual activity. Quite possibly some women who had been involved in this cult were now visiting the infant Christian church in Ephesus, and some of them were demanding to teach their views when they had no business teaching anyone.

How does 1 Timothy 2:13–14 apply to us today, since we are not battling first-century gnosticism? When we view this passage in context, Paul's comments about Eve's deception are a clear warning to us all that we cannot allow the gospel message to be twisted. We cannot compromise the Word of God to accommo-date our culture. We cannot add words to the Bible or take words away. We cannot mix the gospel with occult beliefs. We cannot mingle light with darkness. We must heed the words of the apostle John, who warned the first-century saints: "Guard your-selves from idols" (1 John 5:21).

But we must not misconstrue Paul's words to Timothy to create a doctrine that says women are the source of all deception. That is not the point of this passage. After all, many of the people who were spreading gnosticism in the church at Ephesus were men!

In 1 Timothy 1:20, Paul mentions two false teachers, Hymenaeus and Alexander, men whose blasphemous doctrines had caused them to "suffer shipwreck in regard to their faith." Hymenaeus is mentioned again in Paul's second letter to Timothy, along with another false teacher named Philetus. Noting that their doctrines were spreading "like gangrene" in the church (2 Tim. 2:17), Paul says these men had caused a stir by teaching that the final resurrection had already taken place. And Alexander is described again in 2 Timothy 4:14–15 as a dangerous man who "vigorously opposed" Paul's teachings.

Other unnamed male false teachers mentioned by Paul in 2 Timothy 3 are referred to as "men of depraved mind" (v. 8) and "imposters" (v. 13). Paul notes in verse 6 that these heretics take advantage of "weak women" (probably a reference to blasphe-mous doctrines that encouraged sexual immorality) and compares them to Jannes and Jambres (v. 8), the Egyptian priests who used occult power to oppose Moses in Pharaoh's court. This is most certainly a reference to the fact that the gnostic heretics of the first century had access to a demonic form of magic that produced counterfeit miracles to gain their following.

It is interesting to note that Paul never refers to a female false teacher by name. (The apostle John, however, does mention one in Revelation 2:20.) Most likely, there were some women promoting heretical doctrines in Ephesus, but they certainly were not Paul's major concern. Paul apparently felt that men such as Hymenaeus, Alexander and Philetus represented the greatest threat. The same is true today. While women are certainly as capable as men of inventing strange doctrines, they have never been the major source of deception during any period of church history.

The Power of a Discerning Woman

Some Christians today believe that Paul's message in 1 Timothy 2 implies that Eve was more guilty than Adam when she sinned in the Garden. But no respectable Bible scholar in the church today would promote such a view. The Bible clearly states that Adam and Eve were both held guilty by God for their disobedience, and the consequences of their sin fell equally on both of them.

Also, we need to note that when the concept of original sin is discussed in detail in Paul's epistle to the Romans, he blames Adam, not Eve. We are told that sin entered the world "through the one man's disobedience" (Rom. 5:19) and that sin entered the world "through one man" (v. 12). The texts seem to suggest that while Eve was deceived (and must assume guilt for her deception), Adam sinned with full knowledge of his wrong choice.

The bright side of this, of course, is that the blessings of redemption that were purchased by Jesus Christ are equally available to man and woman. While male and female are helpless to overcome sin without Christ, both are able to obtain forgiveness and restored fellowship with God when they put their trust in the Savior.

If redemption is readily available to women, why then do we continue to block their access to full restoration? Why do Christian men seem to want women to stay under the effects of the curse rather than inviting them to live in the blessings of full redemption? Even if the curse of Eve caused all women to be prone to deception, Christian women can be set free from its power. If the curse of Eve's sin brought degrading treatment by men, then the power of the Holy Spirit can lift women to a new place of dignity and authority.

Although women have inherited the sin nature of their original ancestors, those who experience the transforming power of Christ can rise above the tendency to deceive or be deceived. In fact, God's ultimate plan for His women is that they lead others to the truth. Christian women are not prone to deception; if they are full of the Holy Spirit and have submitted to the process of discipleship, they can teach, preach and lead others into an understanding of the gospel. If the anointing of God abides in them, we have no reason to fear that they will fall into deception simply because they are female.

This point was illustrated for me once in a dream. In my dream, I was walking down a long dark corridor with my wife, Deborah, when suddenly I turned into a stately paneled room that was flanked on all sides by dark wood bookcases. The shelves were filled from top to bottom with old books, and I recognized that most of the volumes were written by famous secular philosophers and occultists. I sensed some danger, but I felt drawn into the musty room because the books seemed so inviting. But as I stepped in, my wife grabbed my arm and pulled me back into the hall.

I awoke suddenly after the dream ended, and I realized that this was the perfect picture of how a Christian woman should respond. God has gifted her with discernment and an intuitive understanding of spiritual things. As she grows in her relationship with Christ, her discerning gifts should become so sharp that she can immediately detect spiritual danger and recognize the presence of anything demonic in her home or ministry. And if she sees her husband, children, friends or pastor heading into spiritual trouble, she should boldly reach out to yank them from danger.

Eve, of course, lacked this discernment. When the serpent

approached her, she was deceived by her senses and carried away by her own lusts. But women who have the presence of Christ in their hearts do not have to follow in Eve's footsteps. Not only can they walk away from the serpent's temptations, but also they can rescue others from his craftiness. This is the spiritual inheritance of all redeemed women.

Chapter 7
Questions for Discussion

1. Many churches today believe that women should not teach or serve in public ministry because women are more easily deceived than men. Have you ever been taught this, and how do you feel about it?

2. Some Christians have taught that Eve was more guilty than Adam when they sinned in the Garden of Eden. How would you respond to this idea?

3. It is possible that thousands of innocent women were killed by the church during medieval times after being falsely accused of witchcraft. How might this atrocity affect the attitudes of women today? Do you know women who have rejected Christianity because they encountered demeaning attitudes in the church toward women?

4. Read 1 Timothy 2:12–14 and explain why Paul refers to the fall of Adam and Eve in this passage. In light of the fact that the church in Ephesus was threatened by strange gnostic doctrines, why did Paul have to explain that Eve, and not Adam, was deceived in the Garden of Eden?

5. Describe a time when God allowed you to use super-natural discernment to detect error or spiritual danger.

The woman taught once, and ruined all. On this account . . . let her not teach. . . . The whole female race transgressed . . . Let her not, however, grieve. God hath given her no small consolation, that of childbearing.[1]

—Early church father John Chrysostom (circa 400 a.d.)

As long as woman is for birth and children, she is different from man as body is from soul. But if she wishes to serve Christ more than the world, then she will cease to be a woman and will be called man.[2]

—Jerome, a revered monk of fourth-century Rome

Women are ashamed to admit this, but Scripture and life reveal that only one woman in thousands has been endowed with the God-given aptitude to live in chastity and virginity. A woman is not fully the master of herself. God fashioned her body so that she should be with a man, to have and to rear children . . . No woman should be ashamed of that for which God made and intended her.[3]

—Martin Luther, in a letter he wrote in 1524

Lie #8
Women can't be fulfilled or spiritually effective without a husband and children.

Leilani Corpus' future was bright. A journalism and political science major at the University of Hawaii in Honolulu, she also served as a senator on the student council and found time to volunteer for two state-level political campaigns. She was outspoken about her faith, yet her non-Christian peers respected her for her spunk and obvious leadership skills. Everyone knew this girl had what it takes to make a big impact on the world.

After her graduation, a group of Christian businessmen approached Leilani about running for a state representative seat. Hawaii needed more evangelical Christians in government, and it was obvious to these men that an articulate young woman of Polynesian descent would appeal to mainstream voters. The men offered to fully fund her campaign if she would agree to move to another district on the island to establish her residence there.

Leilani prayed about the opportunity and sensed that God was calling her to step into the political arena. But before contacting the businessmen's group to say yes, she decided to seek counsel from her pastor's wife—who was one of her best friends. She told the woman the whole story and expected her to be excited. She wasn't.

"I would strongly discourage you from doing that," the woman told Leilani. "You're going to get married one day. God has the perfect husband for you. And then what will that be like? How awkward for your husband if the two of you get married and you are in an important political office. That is not God's way. You are called to be a wife first. That has to be your priority."

Leilani was devastated. She trusted this woman as a confidante and spiritual mother. But her advice ran totally contrary to what Leilani was feeling. Many questions raced through her mind as she drove to her apartment that afternoon. *Why should I turn down this opportunity on the basis that I might get married soon? I am not even dating anyone! I don't even know if I will be married five years from now! Why do I have to order my life around this nebulous event called marriage?*

In the end, Leilani couldn't bring herself to dismiss the advice of her mentor. She told the businessmen she couldn't run for office, and she went back to the drawing board to seek God's will for her life. Her next idea: Perhaps she should enroll in law school.

Again, she sought advice from her pastor's wife. And again, the reaction was negative. "Leilani, that is such a high-powered career that requires so much time away from home," the woman said. "What will you do when you are married? What if you had to go out of town to argue a case? You've got to think about your husband."

"But I don't have a husband!" Leilani protested.

"You will. God has a man for you," the woman said with confidence. "And when you are married you will know that he was God's perfect plan."

Apparently, Leilani surmised, God's perfect plan was *a man*.

In spite of her nagging doubts, Leilani submitted to her friend's advice again. She struggled with feelings of worthlessness after the ordeal, wondering if there was something wrong with her because she didn't fully understand how to fit the mold of the "perfect Christian woman" that more traditional women seemed to enjoy.

But Leilani just didn't match the stereotype. She hated to cook and felt like a caged animal when she was stuck at home alone. She preferred to socialize with her friends at restaurants, host movie nights in her apartment or help organize evangelistic out-reaches on campus.

That evening her thoughts screamed out to God: *Lord, why do I have this desire to make an impact on society when my pastors tell me women don't do that? And why do I have to put my life on hold until I walk down the aisle?*

Fortunately, Leilani didn't bury her dreams. She admits that she put her life on hold for a few years, but when Mr. Right didn't come along she took a journalism job and became a successful freelance writer. It was almost ten years after her pivotal talk with the pastor's wife that Leilani married Jerome—a compassionate man who fully supported her desire to work outside the home as a public relations director for a growing church in Missouri. Today she is training to enter pastoral ministry—and she has a special concern for single women who feel they've been put on the shelf by the church.

The Myth of the "Incomplete" Woman

The advice given to Leilani in the mid-1980s is typical of the line that many Christians impose on single women today. In con-servative churches, women are constantly told that marriage and motherhood are their "God-given roles" in life. While men are exhorted to transform society through full-time ministry or through their Christian witness on the job, women are expected to make the home their primary sphere of influence. It matters little even if economic realities force them into the workplace or if they sense a spiritual calling into a secular profession at which they excel. Single women are told that life begins at the altar. Everything leading up to that moment is simply preparation for "the big day."

Many times, Christian women who are successful in business or in some other professional field feel unwelcome in the church, as if they are an unhealthy influence on women who have more "pure" domestic inclinations. Meanwhile, Christian men—whether single or married—are encouraged to excel in their businesses, and they are never told that their primary role in life is to be a husband or father even though many of them are called to be both.

Lynn Scarborough owns a media consulting firm in Dallas, and she has trained top television news anchors for CNN and other networks. Her advice is sought by media companies, and she has coached high-level executives on how to improve their communication skills. But her conservative church does not know what to do with her. Like Leilani Corpus, Lynn doesn't fit the mold.

"I am allowed to carpool, cater meals and contribute money to the church," Lynn told me. She is not bitter about the way she's been treated, but it has been painful for her to realize that a cultural bias exists in the church toward unmarried women.

Lynn calls it a hidden prejudice, but it manifests itself regularly. Once, a man in the church offered to sponsor a seminar for other businessmen who wanted to enhance their entrepreneurial skills. She challenged him on why he was excluding women from the meeting, since more women than men are starting new businesses in the United States each year. "He looked at me like he had never even thought of women running businesses," Lynn said.

On another occasion, a youth pastor gave a Sunday morning appeal for volunteers to drive buses for an outreach to urban kids. But he asked for help only from the men in the congregation. When Lynn challenged his sexism, asking why women couldn't drive the buses too, he told her that the underprivileged children in this neighborhood needed father figures.

Lynn was made to feel like a spiritual misfit. "I am qualified to be a spiritual mother to kids who are starved for love," Lynn told me. "But I was told that I wasn't qualified, so don't bother. I was also told that I couldn't lead a home fellowship group because I am single. Most churches just haven't figured out how to minister to single career women like me or how to use our spiritual gifts."

Women like Lynn are everywhere in the church today. They are committed disciples of Jesus, but leaders have told them that the best way to serve God is to get married, make their husbands happy and bring lots of children into the world. This is God's "highest assignment" for females, or so they are told. A woman's destiny is to be found in her male partner. She will be forever incomplete without him.

But does the Bible say that every woman is supposed to marry? And if she is, should she put her entire life on hold until she throws her wedding bouquet into the hands of another prospective bride? Why should we encourage single women to waste the most productive years of their lives by waiting for romance, when their unique talents could be harnessed for a holy purpose?

No verse in the Bible says that God's ultimate purpose for a woman is to find a mate and then reproduce. On the contrary, the Scriptures say that our lives can be made complete by only one thing: a constant, abiding relationship with Christ. This is true for men and women alike—all of us are called to know Him. This is our ultimate destiny. Jesus said it plainly:

> And this is life eternal, *that they might know thee* the only true God, and Jesus Christ, whom thou hast sent.
> —JOHN 17:3, KJV, EMPHASIS ADDED

God never intended for a woman to derive her value from a man or to base her worth on producing offspring. Neither marriage nor childbirth validate a woman's personhood, her character or her spirituality. *A Christian woman's identity is to be found in Christ alone.* He makes her complete, whether she has a husband and twelve children or if she remains single all her life. Christ is her life; she is betrothed to Him. To place her husband, her children or any other human relationship above Christ would be idolatry. (See Luke 14:26.)

Of course marriage is ordained by God, and it was meant to be a wonderful blessing that includes romance, sexual intimacy and the deepest expression of human love. Of course God wants husbands to love their wives; of course He wants wives to love their husbands; of course He wants children to thrive in the overflow of this love. But for many people this ideal of the Christian family will never materialize.

When we become His disciples, Jesus doesn't promise that our lives will have romantic, fairy-tale endings. He never promises the single man that he will find a wife who can attain to society's unreasonable standards of beauty or sensuality. Likewise, He doesn't promise the single woman that Prince Charming will sweep her off her feet one day. Jesus calls us to radical obedience. He invites us to "lose our lives" and to die to our own desires—including the desire for intimate companionship. (See John 12:25.)

This is the message we should offer single Christians today. Rather than enticing them to serve the false idols of fulfillment, we need to challenge them to surrender every aspect of their futures to God. He requires us to lay our fleshly romantic fantasies on His altar. He would much rather that we find our full satisfaction in Him than to watch us sell our souls to the world. He wants us to wait for Isaac rather than settle for Ishmael.

The heartcry of every unmarried Christian should be, "Lord, I'm willing to serve you no matter what. Regardless of whether I marry this year or stay single the rest of my life, I'll find my contentment in You." This is the attitude of surrender that God is looking for in every heart.

Married to Christ

For centuries God has been using single women who possessed this rare attitude of total surrender. Of course they wanted to get married, but the right man never came along. These women probably felt lonely; perhaps they were burdened by the intensely painful stigma of being single. But in the midst of this anguish God became the Lover of their souls, and they pressed beyond their pain to explore a realm of spiritual fulfillment that is reserved only for those who pursue Him with abandon.

Teresa of Ávila, a sixteenth-century Spanish nun, wrote volumes about her love relationship with Christ—and today millions have been introduced to a deeper intimacy with God through reading collections of her contemplative prayers. Her message, sharpened through single-hearted devotion, is summed up in one line of a poem she wrote: "Whoever possesses God lacks nothing; God alone suffices."[4]

We should be calling Christians—male and female—to lay aside ambitions and carnal desires to obey God's will no matter the cost. How ridiculous to expect this level of spiritual commitment from men and then to tell women that they should focus their spiritual energies on finding a husband! Women are called to be lovers of God, too. Why should we expect less of them?

We also must stop placing a heavy yoke on unmarried and divorced women in the church by suggesting that they are not complete without a man in their lives or that a husband somehow legitimizes their ministries. Marriage does not qualify anyone to serve in the church. Pastors do not have to be married. We know this because the Bible does not state clearly whether certain key leaders, such as Paul or Timothy, were married or not.

From the time she was released from a German death camp in 1944 until her death in 1983, Corrie ten Boom told the world about a Savior who could forgive the cruelest Nazi. Her testimony of forgiveness, recounted in the book *The Hiding Place,* became a bestseller and an acclaimed motion picture. The story opened up speaking engagements for Corrie in sixty countries. Before she died at age ninety-one, she had established several rehabilitation centers for victims of the Holocaust. Yet this soft-spoken evangelist never married. Did the fact that she didn't have a husband make her less "complete"? No, Corrie found her fulfillment in Christ alone.

Single women have shaken nations for the gospel since the church began. One of the earliest we know of is Macrina, a fourth-century nun who decided to dedicate her life to God's service when her fiancé died. She built one of the first monasteries for women (in what is modern-day Turkey), and she also established a primitive hospital.[5]

The German prophetess Hildegarde (1098–1179) broke the medieval traditions of her day by functioning as a spokesperson for God to Europe's leaders—both in the church and in government. She claimed to have had numerous visions of Christ, and she recorded messages from Him in her most famous book, *Know the Ways of the Lord.* She also wrote seventy popular worship songs and authored the first known morality play. At age sixty she began an itinerant preaching ministry—traveling as far away as France on horseback. She didn't allow her singleness to hold her back from fulfilling her spiritual destiny.[6]

Catherine of Siena (1347–1380) was a courageous prophetess who stood against pride and greed among clergy many years before Martin Luther called for reform in the Roman Catholic church. She preached openly, sometimes to crowds of more than one thousand, in a day when society frowned on women who did any kind of public speaking. In her writings, she says God assured her that He had called her to preach. "Am not I He who created the human race, who formed both man and woman?" God told her. "I pour out the favor of My Spirit on whom I will. Go forth without fear, in spite of reproach. . . . I have a mission for you to fulfill."[7]

After writer Hannah More (1745–1833) was jilted by her fiancé, she moved to London and joined an Anglican community that was active in social reform. Deeply influenced by the famous abolitionist William Wilberforce, More became concerned for the welfare of poor miners and their families. Her growing compassion led her to establish a network of Sunday schools that eventually reached twenty thousand children in England. She didn't allow a failed romance to throw her into a pit of self-centered depression; instead she allowed God to pull her into a place of selfless giving.[8]

Lottie Moon (1840–1912) broke her engagement to a wealthy Virginian because she knew he did not share her Christian convictions. Instead of getting married, she surrendered her life to missionary work in China—serving the Southern Baptist Convention until she died. Although she is best known today for her ability to raise funds, her writings reveal that she was a woman born before her time. Moon was troubled by the obvious sexism she observed in ministry, and she was critical of her male superiors who thought women missionaries should limit their work to teaching children.[9]

Some people told Mary Slessor (1848–1915) that she had no business going to Africa as a missionary. But this red-haired Scottish woman braved sickness and danger to plant churches among the cannibalistic tribes of the Calibar region—in what is now Nigeria. On several occasions Slessor risked her life by challenging tribal customs, which included the beating and even killing of women who had committed trivial offenses. Inspired by the missionary pioneer David Livingstone, Slessor was one of many unmarried European women in the nineteenth century who ventured into unreached nations to plant thriving churches.[10]

Henrietta Mears (1890–1963) had fallen in love with a non-Christian man, but she severed the relationship out of obedience to the Lord and later joined the First Presbyterian Church in Hollywood, California, where she became director of Christian education. The Sunday school grew from four hundred fifty to four thousand in less than three years, and she developed lively lessons that she later published when she founded Gospel Light—one of the most respected publishers of Sunday school literature today. She is best known for mentoring three young men who later reaped huge spiritual harvests: Bill Bright, founder of Campus Crusade for Christ; Richard Halverson, a pastor who later became chaplain of the U.S. Senate; and evangelist Billy Graham.[11]

The millions of people who found Christ through the impact of a Billy Graham television broadcast, or because of Campus Crusade's outreach at a university, owe a huge debt to an unmarried woman named Henrietta Mears. Her culture told her that she needed a man—any man—to bring her fulfillment. But she rejected that lie and chose to find her fulfillment in Christ. She threw herself into the purposes of God for her generation—and it is likely that her obedience produced more spiritual fruit than any other Christian minister of the twentieth century.

The Curse of Eve

Throughout history women have been told that God created them solely for marriage and childbirth. Some respected church fathers, including Martin Luther and John Knox, believed that women were useless in the kingdom of God unless they had babies—since procreation was their only mission in life.

This demeaning view of women as baby-making machines isn't a biblical view, but it does resemble the teachings of Mormons, whose earliest doctrines included the idea that Mormon men should beget as many children as possible to achieve greater glory in heaven. (This is also why Mormons, until 1890, practiced polygamy. They still teach that wives cannot be saved unless they are "called" into heaven by their husbands.)[12]

The ability to have children does not represent a woman's only calling in life, and God never intended her to be defined by her reproductive capacity. Women are not wombs. Yet since the Fall of man in the Garden of Eden, woman has been stripped of her calling to rule with Adam, and as a result she often has been viewed as a sex object, a domestic servant and a childbearer. After Adam and Eve sinned, God told the woman that her ability to reproduce would become a painful burden to bear rather than a blessing. He said in Genesis 3:16:

> I will greatly multiply your pain in childbirth, in pain you shall bring forth children; yet your desire shall be for your husband, and he shall rule over you.

This reference to "pain in childbirth" speaks of much more than the anguish of labor and delivery. This passage also alludes to the lifelong hardships that would accompany all women after the fall. God was saying that because of sin, pain would rule women's lives.

Their femininity would be marred in many ways. Being female would become a burden. They might be raped or molested. They might be sold into prostitution, as are many young girls in Thailand today. Their genitals might be mutilated, a barbaric practice that is imposed on hundreds of thousands of girls in Africa today. They might suffer from domestic violence. Their husbands might even kill them in revenge for "shaming their honor"—as many Muslim men are permitted to do today in some Middle Eastern countries.

The "pain of childbirth" would result in unbelievable tragedy and heartache. Many women would conceive and then lose their babies to miscarriage. They might have babies, and then watch them die prematurely from childhood diseases. They might have baby girls, and then watch in horror as these infants are killed by societies that place greater value on males (as is common today in parts of India). As many women in the United States do, they might watch their children grow up to become cocaine addicts or criminals.

And—worst of all—they might kill their own children through abortion. The death toll caused by abortion in the twentieth century (more than 1.3 billion unborn babies killed throughout the world since 1973, according to the National Right to Life Committee) is surely evidence of the unimaginable toll of original sin.

This was the curse of Eve!

As a result of sin, woman would not be esteemed as a co-equal with man but would be treated as an inferior. Her husband would expect her to serve him and submit to his every whim. She would not be defined by her character or her worth in God's eyes but by her physical beauty. She would be viewed by men as a sex object—not respected as a daughter of God. She would be stripped of her dignity, despised, ignored, mistreated, blamed, harassed and denied opportunities.

This has been the fate of women since the Garden. In ancient Greece, philosophers, including Plato and Aristotle, taught that women actually were a lower animal species. Plato believed that women were a degenerate form of manly perfection, and that men who did not live righteous lives would be reincarnated as females.[13]

Aristotle held equally strange views about sexual reproduction. Because men produce semen and women do not, Aristotle reasoned that men had the godlike quality to create life while "defective" women could provide only the "matter" necessary in which to grow human life.[14] In other words, man provides the precious seed; the woman provides nothing more than the nourishing soil. Man creates life; woman simply offers a place for this miracle of life to develop. Man is a god in his creative power; woman is just an incubator. They did not yet understand the scientific truth that reproduction requires life-giving cells from both males and females.

Because women in ancient times were considered the property of their husbands, the womb of woman was considered man's domain. If he wanted to produce fifteen children, it was his prerogative. His wife had no say in the matter. Childbirth was the very reason for her existence. If she died while giving birth, her husband could find another womb to impregnate. Childbirth was her fate, and if she gave birth to daughters, it was their fate as well.

But Jesus Christ changed all of this! He never intended for women to continue to labor under this horrible curse. He paid the full price for sin. Women no longer bear the guilt of Adam and Eve.

When women are free in Christ, they are restored to the place of equality and dignity that belonged to Eve before the Fall. They can walk on this earth in the favor and blessings of God. They can exercise the authority of Christ. They are no longer slaves to sin. They are no longer subject to the curse of mistreatment and abuse by sinful men. Redeemed women receive the grace to function as equals—with loving husbands who love them as Christ loves the church.

And in Christ, women are not baby-making machines. They are not defined through biology. Although they may marry and have children, their purpose and destiny are not limited to the natural realm. They are elevated, with all the saints, to a place of communion with Christ in the spiritual realm—a place where the curse of sin cannot be found.

The Triumph of the Incarnation

In conservative churches in the United States, some Christians have twisted one obscure passage in the New Testament to suggest that women must give birth to children in order to be saved or to be spiritually effective. This is an absurd notion, of course— one that contradicts the Bible's message of free grace in Christ. Nevertheless, it is important that we examine this passage:

> For it was Adam who was first created, and then Eve. And it was not Adam who was deceived, but the woman being quite deceived, fell into transgression. *But women shall be preserved* [or literally "saved"] *through the bearing of children if they continue in faith and love and sanctity with self-restraint.*
> —1 TIMOTHY 2:13–15, EMPHASIS ADDED

Surely Paul was not issuing a guarantee that Christian women would never die in childbirth. And of course we know that Paul was not implying that women must have children to be accepted in Christ. Where would that leave unmarried women or those who are barren? Paul devoted much of his New Testament writings to refuting the notion that salvation can be obtained by works. He boldly proclaimed to the Jewish legalists that only faith in the atonement of Christ brings true conversion. So what can this verse possibly mean?

Bible scholars are not in agreement about this passage, and

many confess they don't understand its complexities. Richard and Catherine Clark Kroeger suggest that the passage is written to oppose a gnostic heresy, popular in Ephesus in the first century, that instructed women to deny their femininity to find salvation. So Paul, contradicting the false teachers, could be reaffirming that women do not need to change their sexual identity or renounce their childbearing ability to know Christ.[15]

There is another possible translation of 1 Timothy 2:15, however, that makes more sense. Some scholars believe the Greek text points to the coming of the Messiah through the virgin Mary. The verse could be translated in this way: "But women will be saved through the bearing of *the Child*..." Another reading could be: "She shall be saved by (or through) *the Childbearing*..." This interpretation was the view of pioneer missionary and Bible expositor Katherine Bushnell. In her 1923 book *God's Word to Women,* she states clearly what Paul was saying to Timothy:

> Women are not saved from death in childbirth, nor are they spiritually saved merely by the animal process of giving birth to children. Women are saved from their sins, and are saved for heaven precisely on the same terms as men, and on no additional terms; for God is no respecter of persons. What Paul says here, as literally translated from the Greek, is, 'She [woman] shall be saved by the childbearing,'—that is, by the birth of a Redeemer into the world.[16]

In other words, even though women came under a curse of degradation as a result of sin in the Garden of Eden, the promised Messiah—the Christchild—came to reverse this curse and bring women into a place of redemption and transformation. Christ's miraculous incarnation, which occurred through the faith of a young Jewish maiden named Mary, would forever release women from the weight of Eve's sin.

The miracle of Christ's incarnation was actually proclaimed by God in the Garden after Adam and Eve fell. The Lord said to the serpent:

> And I will put enmity between you and the woman, and between your seed and her seed; he shall bruise you on the head, and you shall bruise him on the heel.
>
> —Genesis 3:15

This first biblical prophecy foretells of a day when *the seed of woman*—Jesus Christ, born of a virgin yet God incarnate—would defeat the serpent forever and bring full restoration of God's kingdom to earth. While it was a woman, Eve, who was first tempted to listen to Satan's voice, God promised that another woman, Mary, would miraculously conceive "'the holy offspring'" when she was overshadowed by "'the power of the Most High.'" (See Luke 1:35.)

Eve listened to the serpent and became his slave. Mary, when approached by the angel, believed God's Word and gave birth to the Deliverer—who would ultimately cast the serpent into the abyss forever. This sinless Messiah, although born of a woman, was not tainted by the sin of Adam and Eve. And for that reason He was able to plunder hell and secure eternal life for all who trust Him.

Because of the incarnation, women are liberated from the pains of sin that have marred them for centuries. Now elevated to a place of dignity in Christ, they are also, like Mary, called to be life-givers—not just of natural offspring, but of spiritual fruit. Women who are restored to a right relationship with God and are filled with His Spirit can trample on the enemy's head, too.

Married or single, with children or without, women are called into His presence where they can be overshadowed by His power just as Mary was. As partners with Him, they too can release mighty deliverance. They can win the lost, heal the sick and cast out demons. They can reach neighborhoods or impact entire nations. They can serve as pastors, teachers, evangelists, prophets, apostles and missionaries. No longer in bondage to Eve's legacy, they are free to find their identity in the One who canceled the curse forever.

Chapter 8
Questions for Discussion

1. Discuss how you feel single women are treated in your church. Why do you think some Christians feel single women should make marriage a priority rather than pursuing a career path?

2. Why is it so important for a single Christian to surrender all desires related to romance and marriage? How does a person walk out this attitude of surrender?

3. List some of the effects that the curse of sin, mentioned in Genesis 3:16, has had on women throughout the world. How did the coming of Christ reverse this curse?

4. Discuss possible interpretations of 1 Timothy 2:15. Why is it contrary to the heart of the gospel to suggest that women must have babies in order to be saved?

Men have broad shoulders and narrow hips, and accordingly they possess intelligence. Women have narrow shoulders and broad hips. Women ought to stay at home; the way they were created indicates this, for they have broad hips and a wide fundament to sit upon, keep house and bear and raise children.[1]

—MARTIN LUTHER

Remain in your houses and gates unless you have something of importance to regulate, such as to make purchases, to provide in temporal needs, to hear the Word of the Lord, or to receive the holy sacraments, etc. Attend faithfully to your charge, to your children, house, and family...[2]

—A MESSAGE TO WOMEN FROM ANABAPTIST LEADER
MENNO SIMONS (1496–1561)

Many women will be so busy about voting and political office that the home and children will have no attraction for them, and American mothers and children, like Christian charity, will be a rarity.[3]

THE LUTHERAN WITNESS,
IN AN 1894 EDITORIAL OPPOSING WOMEN VOTING

Lie **#9**
Women shouldn't work outside the home.

In the small town of Berryville, in northwest Arkansas, members of the board at First Baptist Church voted in February 1997 to close their church-run day-care center. They made the abrupt decision not because the facility was too expensive to operate or because they didn't have enough children enrolled. The official reason, as stated in a letter that was mailed to parents, was that church leaders felt their day-care center was encouraging women to work outside the home.

"God intended for the home to be the center of a mother's world," the letter from First Baptist stated, adding that working moms "neglect their children, damage their marriages and set a bad example." First Baptist's day-care center board, under the direction of the pastor, also noted in their letter that families should learn to get by on the husband's single income and that this might mean they would have to forfeit "big TVs, a microwave, new clothes, eating out and nice vacations." (One wonders if the men who voted on this policy ever ate at restaurants, bought new suits or used microwave ovens.)

The day-care center closed one month later as the parents scrambled to find another place to leave these twenty-seven children. Arkansas state officials, in fact, had to get involved; they were relieved to find another church in town that was willing to organize a day-care program.

First Baptist's decision was not warmly welcomed by everyone in the community. One woman whose daughter had been enrolled in the day-care center told the Associated Press that she felt the church wanted everyone in Berryville to pretend they lived in the 1950s. "I don't know of too many people here who can survive on one person's salary, especially if that salary is minimum wage," the woman said. "This is just something that shouldn't have happened in this decade."[4]

What did this church accomplish by telling women they should forfeit vacations and stay home with their kids in order to please God? Perhaps some of the wives whose husbands had jobs considered staying home a viable option. The single mothers most likely either laughed in disbelief or cried in desperation when they received the shocking letter. Staying home to cook, clean house and do laundry all day was not an option for them. They had mouths to feed, and the church was not offering to mail them a weekly paycheck. The only thing the church offered these women was an extra dose of condemnation by telling them they were neglecting their children by working.

So, is it any wonder that so many people—and an increasing number of women—have rejected the church? Is this a viable strategy for evangelizing the working women of the new millennium—by telling them they are living in sin because they are pursuing a career? I don't think so.

The leaders of First Baptist of Berryville were totally out of touch with the needs of the women in their community, and thankfully they didn't trigger a trend of day-care center closings when news of their decision made national headlines. But the sad fact is that the mind-set that led the men of this church to act so irrationally is common in the evangelical church today. We may live in the twenty-first century, but eighteenth-century ideas about women's roles are still embedded in our minds—

and leaders twist and misinterpret the Bible to defend this view.

The "women shouldn't work" argument comes in various forms. The mildest variety—and the one that actually makes sense in some situations—states that God intends for a wife to nurture her children while they are young and that she should let her husband provide the bulk of family income during those years. This line of reasoning works for some families in wealthier Western countries, and many women in the United States enjoy playing with their toddlers at home all day while daddy is at the office. Some women even choose to homeschool their children due to concerns about the values being promoted in public education or because academic standards in public schools are often poor.

In 1999, it was estimated that eight million American women were full-time, stay-at-home mothers. In their book *And What Do You Do?*, written from a secular perspective, authors Mary A. Quigley and Loretta Kaufman argue that many educated, professional women today are choosing to be full-time moms during their children's young years. Many of these women choose this path not for religious reasons but because they are concerned about the quality of day care or the threat of school violence, or simply because they want to spend more time with their kids.[5]

There is certainly nothing wrong with this stay-at-home-mother scenario. In fact, many child-development experts—both Christian and secular—believe that having a parent or close relative at home all day during the most formative years is a major factor in producing well-adjusted kids. The Bible does not say the stay-at-home mom is the norm for all families, nor does it place all the burden of childcare on the wife. But it certainly is a blessing when finances allow children to receive this kind of nurturing.

Things get more complicated for families when they cannot survive on one income. There are millions of two-parent families that struggle to pay their bills, especially if the father works at a factory, a convenience store or a construction site. The wife is often forced to find at least a part-time job while she juggles childcare responsibilities. And then there are many single mothers who must work even if they qualify for partial welfare benefits. Perhaps because of their own wrong choices, abandonment or social disadvantages these women struggle constantly to balance the pressures of home and work.

They should be able to turn to the church for moral support and spiritual resources. But often what we offer them is a slap in the face. We often quote to them Titus 2:4:

> Encourage the young women to love their husbands, to love their children, to be sensible, pure, *workers at home.*
>
> —EMPHASIS ADDED

Then we twist this verse to say that God requires all women to fit into the cookie-cutter mold of the full-time Christian house-wife. We also tell women in the church that they should model their lives after the "virtuous woman" (KJV) described in Proverbs 31—and then we misread that passage to imply that she too was a stay-at-home mother. But that is not what the Scripture says.

First of all, we need to understand that the Proverbs 31 woman was never meant to be interpreted as normative for every Christian woman. The Hebrew poetry employed in this passage of Proverbs is an acrostic; each verse begins with a different letter of the Hebrew alphabet and describes some aspect of a godly woman's life.

The "woman" described here is actually a composite—the passage was never meant to describe one woman. (If it were, she would indeed be an Old Testament superwoman, since she never seems to sleep or stop working!) Christian women who uphold the Proverbs 31 woman as a virtuous ideal must realize that God does not expect them to emulate her unrealistic schedule—because she is actually several "model" women rolled into one.

But even if we view this woman as one individual, we need to recognize that her work was not limited to domestic chores. She was a shrewd businesswoman who was involved in real estate, agriculture and a textile business. She also employed other women to help her. The text tells us:

> She looks for wool and flax, and works with her hands in delight....She considers a field and buys it; from her earn-ings she plants a vineyard....She stretches out her hand to

the distaff, and her hands grasp the spindle....She makes
linen garments and sells them, and supplies belts to the
tradesmen.

—PROVERBS 31:13, 16, 19, 24

Traditionalists who champion this verse as a picture of the
happy housewife would probably not endorse the lifestyle of this
woman if they met her on the street. In her ancient Middle
Eastern society, she was an entrepreneur. She stayed occupied
with her home-based business day and night—and someone else
probably watched her children when she was selling linen in the
marketplace, dealing with merchants, buying fields or making
wine with the fruit of her vineyard. She was most definitely not a
stay-at-home mom in the suburban American sense of the word.
Those who use this passage to keep women locked into an exclusively domestic role are misusing Scripture to hold women in a
crippling form of religious bondage.

Did Paul Tell Women to Stay Home?

Fundamentalist Christians in the United States have long con-
tended that God's highest plan for woman is to function as a
housewife—content to iron clothes, cook casseroles, diaper
babies, bathe toddlers and perhaps master the fine art of sewing
or embroidery while the children are napping. That's because we
have viewed the Bible through a warped cultural lens and have
imposed on the Scriptures our suburban American values and
prejudice. When this view is questioned, conservative Christians
often cite Titus 2:4–5 as well as 1 Timothy 5:14:

> Therefore, I want younger widows to get married, bear chil-
> dren, *keep house*, and give the enemy no occasion for reproach.
> —1 TIMOTHY 5:14, EMPHASIS ADDED

If we examine these two New Testament verses closely, it is
obvious that what the apostle Paul was demanding of women was
not domesticity but *Christian faithfulness.* He was not discour-
aging women from working outside the home. How do I know
this? *Because the concept of going to work was not an option for*

women in the first century. Paul's concern had nothing to do with women leaving their homes to pursue careers—*because women in the agrarian society of Crete in the year* A.D. *62 didn't do that!*

Rebecca Merrill Groothuis, in her 1994 book *Women Caught in the Conflict,* says the notion of the ideal Christian family that we promote today—the view that the father goes to work while the wife stays home with the children—is a view that did not develop until the nineteenth century. It certainly was not the norm for society in Bible times.[6]

In the 1800s, before the Industrial Revolution, both men and women worked at home. Most people farmed, fished or hunted; if they had a trade, their workplace was situated somewhere on their property or in their own house. Men did not get up each morning and go to work after drinking their coffee; their wives did not kiss them at the door and wait for them to return at dinner time. In most cases, both the husband and the wife worked from dawn until dusk at their home-based business: They made cloth, tended animals, smelted metal, fashioned leather, harvested crops or made pottery while their children played at their feet. This was the norm for most families for hundreds of years.

And Groothuis points out that women in agrarian societies worked as hard or harder than their husbands: "Mothers as well as fathers had economically necessary work to do, so mothers were not necessarily preoccupied with child care. Children were cared for by older children and members of the extended family. Women did not organize their lives around their children to any great extent. The definition of motherhood as a full-time job did not exist."[7]

We must be careful not to read *into* the Bible something that isn't there. We can't use Paul's instructions to the Christian women of Ephesus and Crete to concoct a doctrine about men's and women's roles. Paul was not talking about roles in either of these passages. He was addressing serious issues of character.

When he mentions the issue of "keeping house" in 1 Timothy 5:14, Paul was encouraging married female converts to view with seriousness their responsibilities as wives and mothers.

In Titus 1:12, Paul mentions that the people of Crete were

known for their laziness. Their pagan culture was crumbling because men and women were enslaved to drunkenness, gluttony and debauchery. It is possible that many of the men in Crete didn't work at all—perhaps they spent most of their lives drinking in their huts. Perhaps the women were living in this kind of stupor as well. So naturally when they embraced the message of Christ and joined the fledgling churches that Titus was overseeing, one of Paul's first priorities as an apostle was to disciple them in areas of personal conduct, family life and basic self-control.

Paul told the men of Crete to learn to be temperate. (See Titus 2:2.) They needed to break ties with their past and leave their alcoholism, promiscuity and slothfulness behind. Likewise, he told the women to learn to "keep house." Most likely the women were horrible at managing their domestic affairs—and they were neglecting their children in the process. In order to please God and be credible witnesses in their culture, these women would have to change the way they lived. They would have to discipline their unruly children. They would have to love them rather than neglect them. They would have to bring order where there had been domestic chaos.

When we examine 1 Timothy 5:14, we see that Paul expressed concerns about laziness among the women of Ephesus. He says in verse 13 that they are idle and that many of them had become "gossips and busybodies." So naturally his remedy for their problem was to urge them to become women of virtue and integrity. He instructed them to stay home (rather than wasting time spreading rumors and silly talk) and to maintain order in their homes. In fact, the word used in this passage for "keep house" is the same word used for a ruler or master. Yet, translators, perhaps because they were uncomfortable giving women a sense of authority, translated this phrase "keep house" rather than "rule their homes." (The one exception is the Revised Standard Version, which translates 1 Timothy 5:14: "So I would have younger widows marry, bear children, rule their households. . . . ")

Disorder and unfaithfulness in the homes of the Ephesian converts were serious issues for Paul. When he listed the qualifications of an overseer in 1 Timothy 3:1–7, he wrote:

If a man does not know how to manage his own household,
how will he take care of the church of God?

—1 TIMOTHY 3:5

In essence he says, "The Christian life must start at home. Get
your own life in order. Get your marriage in order. Get your children in order. After you've done that, then you will have something of value to take to the world."

This is a hard-core truth from the Bible that has universal appli-
cation to us today. When we come to Christ, His transforming
power should change our behavior at home. It should change
alcoholics into sober, hard-working individuals. It should change
cavalier women-chasers into faithful husbands who treat their
wives with respect. And it should change self-absorbed, undisci-
plined women into diligent disciples of Jesus Christ.

But we cannot use these verses to imply that Paul's command
to "keep house" or to be "workers at home" requires that all
Christian women in the twenty-first century stay in their kitchens
all day or shun their God-ordained career paths. Those who teach
this view impose a cruel and legalistic burden on women that isn't
supported by Scripture. We need to stop teaching it and release
Christian women to follow the Holy Spirit's leading with regard
to their callings and careers.

Yes, God wants women to have personal integrity and to bring
order in their families. Yes, He wants them to view motherhood
as a serious responsibility. But that does not prevent them from
becoming doctors, lawyers, entrepreneurs, artists, writers, politi-
cians, scientists—or ordained ministers. God never intended for
women to be barred from such professions.

Of course, a Christian must submit his or her career plans to
the will and guidance of the Holy Spirit. Women who feel called
to the workplace or who simply must work to provide income
need to seek the Lord's direction. They must resist the temptation
to be controlled by ambition, materialism or selfishness.

Some married women who feel called to pursue a career may
sense God is requiring them to put their desires on a back burner
until their children are older. For others, the Lord may provide a

practical alternative for childcare that does not put the youngsters at risk. And in some cases, a husband may even feel called to stay home with the children during those early years.

For married couples, the issue is never one of choosing "roles." What is important is that the husband and wife listen to God together and come to mutual agreement about the way they decide to handle their childcare dilemma.

Can a woman have a full-time job and still demonstrate faithfulness as a mother? Of course. Conversely, is it also possible for a stay-at-home mother to be completely unfaithful in her duties as a wife and mother? Absolutely. Her presence inside the house is not the issue. Her obedience to God is the key.

Breaking the Mold

Where did we get this idea that Christian women must live in the confines of their homes all day in order to please God? This view is not taught in the Bible—although it is taught rigidly by Muslims, who also insist that women must wear veils. Some Muslims, in fact, believe it is a sin for a woman to be seen at all except by her husband. She must be closeted as a slave in a system that holds some five hundred million women in captivity in the world today.

The God of the Bible does not require women to remain housebound. Jesus Christ sets people free from the prison of sin; His message was never meant to put people in confinement. The gospel sets us free to "go into all the world"; it liberates us—male and female—to do mighty exploits in the name of Jesus. The liberating message we Christians preach in the twenty-first century should never resemble the message of Islam!

But during the last one hundred years, Christians have developed a theory of the traditional family that has required women to conform to a false standard of domesticity. How did this view emerge?

As mentioned earlier, for hundreds of years the traditional family followed the agrarian model: Father and mother worked from sunrise to sunset, scraping out an existence on the family farm or through a home-based trade. Wives walked long distances to fetch water; they worked in the fields and spun their own fabric to make clothes. Children often were cared for by relatives or were left alone to fend for themselves. Older children were put to work as soon as they were physically able.

Then, in the 1800s, came the Industrial Revolution, which led to the creation of what we know today as offices and business districts in Victorian England. Men began to take jobs that required them to leave their homes and families behind. Because of gender bias, women were discouraged from entering the man's world of work. And at that point a new view of women began to emerge among the British middle class: the idea that woman is a weak, delicate individual who must be "protected" from the cruelties of society by staying indoors.[8] It was middle class and very sexist.

This chauvinistic ideal of woman was not a biblical view by any means, but it was adopted by Christians at that time—and has infected the church ever since. Women were told it was not proper for them to venture into the professional world (since they were not smart enough or strong enough), yet they were encouraged to exert "moral influence" on society through more behind-the-scenes methods: by raising godly children and subtly prodding their husbands toward Christian virtue.

Like the tight-fitting corsets women wore in those days, this restrictive view of Christian womanhood demanded that women look beautiful for their husbands—even if the tightness of their underwear restricted their breathing. Women were expected to develop an indoor world that consisted of reading, sewing, cooking, ladies' teas and domestic chores. Their role in life was to bear as many children as possible and then to train them—with little input from their husbands. A woman's highest calling was to create a safe refuge for her man.

But because Christian women of that era began to read, and their reading led to more study, they eventually realized that the whole Victorian mind-set was a cruel hoax. Women in the mid-1800s had a corporate wake-up call and realized that their world was being controlled by men who viewed females as subordinates. And thus the seeds of modern feminism sprouted—as women demanded the right to attend college, vote, be given job opportunities and receive fair wages.

Many Christians today tend to think of the feminist movement as being inherently evil—because modern feminists in the secular arena have focused much of their rhetoric on issues such as abortion and homosexuality. But the earliest leaders of the women's suffrage movement—which secured the passage of the nineteenth amendment to the U.S. Constitution on August 26, 1920, giving women the right to vote—were Bible-believing Christian women who viewed their cause as one of biblical justice.

Lucretia Mott, considered the mother of women's suffrage, was a brave Quaker who became a public speaker when she got involved in the movement to free black slaves. Mott harbored runaway slaves in her home and called Americans to support full emancipation. But after attending an international anti-slavery convention in London in 1840, she realized that her African brethren were not the only ones in bondage. She realized that women, too, must be freed. Eight years later, she and four friends began the women's rights movement during a two-day meeting at a Methodist church in Seneca Falls, New York.

Mott died in 1880, a full forty years before American women won the right to vote. But she sowed the seeds of a Christian awakening, and her lectures on the subject bore little resemblance to modern secular feminism. Her writings were filled with references to great Bible women such as Deborah, Huldah and Phoebe. She frequently quoted the prophet Joel and his prediction that "sons *and daughters* will prophesy." In a speech in 1849, she rebuked those who were attempting to quash discussion of women's rights, and she told them they "preferred darkness to light."

Said Mott: "Free discussion upon this, as upon all other subjects, is never to be feared. Those only who are in the wrong dread discussion. The light alarms those only who feel the need of darkness." Then she quoted Jesus' words in John 3:21, "He that doeth truth cometh to the light, that his deeds may be made manifest, that they are wrought in God" (KJV).[9]

It is a tragedy that the fire that burned in the heart of Lucretia Mott and other Christian suffragists from that era has gone out. Their writings, though well-preserved, have been neglected. Most modern Christians don't even realize that feminism began as a Christian movement. And the established church, which up until

1920 vigorously opposed the idea of women voting, still resists the total spiritual liberation of women. Why?

Part of our hesitancy is fear. Modern believers see non-Christian feminists marching in the streets, campaigning for abortion rights or a radical lesbian agenda. Because we know that homosexuality and baby killing are incompatible with Christianity, we assume that all feministic efforts, both past and present, are unchristian. Sadly, we conclude that any effort to free women from the traditional Christian role of wife and stay-at-home mother is a devilish plot.

We also are guilty of idolizing our narrow, self-made views of the "ideal" Christian family. When these cultural views are challenged, we automatically assume that the devil is at work. We declare that God wants every Christian mother to stay at home full time, and then we interpret anything that doesn't fit this narrow mold as a conspiracy from hell. The real conspiracy, however, is the one Satan has launched to hold women back from achieving their full potential in God.

Let's stop worrying about secular feminists. They are not the real problem, and many of them may actually love God or sincerely want to know Him. What we need to expose is the devil-inspired plot to keep Christian women in a place of subjugation, so they can be released from spiritual bondage and begin to influence our society for righteousness as never before.

Jesus wants His witnesses everywhere. We need godly women in the workplace. We need godly women in government. We need godly women in the media, in the arts and in every profession. How can we be "the light of the world" if we take half the light we have and hide it under a bushel? (See Matthew 5:14.)

What If All Women Stayed Home?

I believe I've heard all the traditionalist arguments for why women should make their homes their primary focus. During the suffrage movement at the beginning of the twentieth century, some Christian denominations predicted that the American family would collapse if women began voting and becoming involved in politics. More recently, I've heard prominent Christian leaders theorize that the decline in morality in our nation is the result of women heading to the workplace. And I've heard a Christian family expert say that if a woman works, her husband's sense of manhood is undermined (because he cannot be the sole provider). Thus his frustration creates unwanted strife in the marriage.

So let's imagine for a moment what the world would be like if women never ventured outside their homes, never pursued careers, never dared to influence anyone outside their own families. We're talking about a world run solely by men—with no women in political office, no women in the health professions, no women leading reform movements, no women working to change the world and no women in the pulpit.

Would you want to live in a world like that? Personally, I think it would be a nightmare.

In this male-dominated world, writer Harriett Beecher Stowe (1811–1896) would not have authored *Uncle Tom's Cabin*—the book that prompted the abolitionist movement, which eventually ended slavery in the United States. Stowe came from a religious family and was probably discouraged from working outside the home. But because her family struggled to live on her husband's meager teacher's salary she decided to make extra money with her serialized novel. She was the first woman in this country to make her living as an author.[10]

If women didn't venture outside their homes, reform leader Jane Addams (1860–1935) would not have moved to the slums of Chicago in 1889 to begin her campaign to change the nation's child labor laws. She wouldn't have challenged unsafe work conditions in factories or worked to solve the problems of juvenile delinquency. And she wouldn't have won the Nobel Peace Prize in 1931.[11]

If women never dared to change the world, Clara Barton (1821–1912) would never have left her home to become a Civil War nurse. And she certainly wouldn't have established the American Red Cross—an organization that today funnels millions of dollars of relief aid to disaster victims.[12]

It was a woman scientist, Alice Evans (1881–1975), whose concern for American children led her to identify the bacterial organism that causes undulant fever. As a researcher with the Department of Agriculture in Washington, Evans was suspicious that spoiled milk was the cause of certain ailments. When she published her findings in 1917 and called for government regulations on the pasteurizing of milk, the dairy industry fought her aggressively. But by the 1930s laws were enacted that required pasteurization.[13]

It was a woman, Rachael Carson (1907–1964), who stopped the use of the deadly pesticide known as DDT. A trained zoologist, she became concerned about the impact of pesticides on animals after some birds in her neighborhood died suddenly. She gave birth to the modern ecology movement with her 1962 book *Silent Spring,* which called for the regulation of pesticides. Because of her groundbreaking research, DDT was banned in the United States a few years after her death.[14]

The list of scientific achievements by women in the last century is astonishing. Gerty Radnitz Cori received the Nobel prize in science in 1947 after documenting how glucose is converted to glycogen—a discovery that aided the treatment of people with diabetes. Florence Seibert was a Yale University-trained medical researcher who pioneered the first accurate test for tuberculosis. College professor Nettie Stevens discovered that the x and y chromosomes determine the gender of humans.[15] Gertrude Elian won the Nobel prize in 1988 for creating drugs that successfully fight childhood leukemia; she also created an immune system-sustaining drug that allows doctors to perform organ transplants.

Would we want to live in a world where these women hadn't been allowed to make their discoveries? We need to remember that most of the women who made early breakthroughs in American medicine were originally barred from attending medical school because of their gender. One of them, Virginia Apgar (1909–1974), successfully convinced obstetricians to focus more of their attention on infants during the labor and delivery process. She developed what is known today as "the Apgar Scale," which measures the health of infants by such factors as skin color, pulse and respiration.[16] (One wonders if a man would have shared her concern for babies.)

And what about the hundreds of Christian women who broke the mold during the last one hundred years and bravely dared to step into the ministry—at a time when doing so was extremely unpopular? What would the world be like if the great women preachers of the holiness movement in the late 1800s—women such as Phoebe Palmer or Maria Woodworth-Etter—had not traveled across the country winning souls? What if Catherine Booth had not been involved in the founding of the Salvation Army? What if Baptist pioneer missionaries such as Lottie Moon had never headed to the mission field because it was not "their place" to leave the home?

There is a world to win for Christ, and too often the church has told half of our volunteers that they can't enlist. Let's break the molds and tear down the barriers. We need women on the front lines.

Chapter 9
Questions for Discussion

1. Discuss the decision made by First Baptist Church of Berryville, Arkansas. How do you view their 1997 vote to close their day-care center?

2. Study the words of Paul in 1 Timothy 5:14 and Titus 2:5. What did Paul mean when he encouraged women to "keep house" and become "workers at home"?

3. Read Proverbs 31:10–31. In what ways does this "virtuous woman" break the mold of a "stay-at-home" mother?

4. Discuss your opinion of the modern feminist movement. In what ways has it veered off course from its beginnings as a Christian movement?

5. Christian women are sometimes stigmatized as being "out of God's will" if they are involved in a profession—especially if they have young children. Discuss your feelings about this. Do you think the Bible prohibits mothers from working outside the home when their children are small? What advice would you give a woman who is wrestling with this decision?

*Take up a stick and beat her, not in rage, but out of charity
and concern for her soul, so that the beating will
rebound to your merit and her good.*[1]

—Friar Cherubino in his *Rules of Marriage*,
on what a medieval husband should do if his wife
does not obey his verbal correction

---

*Woman must neither begin nor complete anything
without man: Where he is, there she must be, and bend
before him as before a master, whom she shall fear and to
whom she shall be subject and obedient.*[2]

—Martin Luther

---

*Women with a violent spouse have believed that the
Bible actually says what they have been taught it says—
that women are inferior in status before husband and God
and deserving of a life of pain.*[3]

—Boston University theology professor
Susan Brooks Thistlethwaite

Lie #10
Women must obediently submit to their husbands in all situations.

A few years ago, *Charisma* magazine reporter Marcia Ford set out to uncover the reason so much spouse abuse occurs in evangelical and charismatic churches. She was aware of the statistics: An estimated four million women are assaulted each year by their current or former spouses. She also had reason to believe that many Christian women were victims in this national trend. But she was surprised to learn, after talking with the director of a prominent counseling clinic, that many of the calls that came into the Rapha Treatment Center's hot line in Dallas not only were from Christians—they were from pastors' wives who said their minister husbands were beating them.[4]

Though the church has been successful at justifying this abuse, or hiding it, one study Ford discovered while doing her research said that pastors typically did not know how to help women who were being abused by their Christian husbands. In a survey of battered women who successfully escaped their abusers, the women who sought help from pastors were usually told to (1) continue to submit to their husbands and (2) pray for the men that they would stop the abusive behavior. It's no wonder the women ranked clergy last in their ability to provide any helpful guidance.

The church has, unknowingly, created an environment that encourages abuse. We cite familiar Bible passages demanding that wives submit to their husbands without providing any explanation of what submission means in a practical sense and without outlining what these same biblical passages demand of husbands. Our counseling has been illogical and irresponsible.

Take, for example, the story of Doris,* a middle-aged woman who attended an Assemblies of God church in the Northeast with her husband, Edward.* Although he was the church's head deacon and was respected by the pastor and the congregation, Edward was privately abusing his wife. For no apparent reason he would erupt into a fit of rage after coming home from work, slapping or hitting Doris in the face so often that she learned to master the art of covering her bruises with makeup.

Doris lived in a prison of inner turmoil. She didn't dare tell anyone at the church about her husband's irrational behavior. She kept trying to appease him. She assumed that one day she would discover what was making him angry and that she would then be able to adjust her own behavior so he wouldn't explode.

Finally, after several serious episodes of violence, she told her pastor. He didn't really believe the abuse was that serious, and he told her she needed to submit.

"He's your husband. You can't just leave him," the pastor said. "It's his house. You're his wife. He has authority over you. You must be making him angry."

Doris was devastated. The pastor had confirmed her worst nightmare. He told her that she was the reason her husband was abusive. It was her fault! On two other occasions Doris returned for pastoral counseling, hoping that perhaps the pastor would change his opinion. On one occasion she expressed sincere fears for her life.

"Don't worry," the pastor said. "Even if you died you would go to be with the Lord. So you win either way. Just keep praying for him. But you are not allowed to leave."

A friend of mine named Nancie finally counseled with Doris

*Not real name.

and realized how serious the situation had become. She told her to get out of the house immediately, but by then Doris had almost no resolve left. She had been brainwashed into thinking that she was worthless and that her life would be over if she left this man who didn't love her.

Nancie begged Doris to move to a shelter or to a friend's house. But Doris politely declined—and repeated what her pastor had told her. "I know I don't have the right to leave him," she said.

Nancie moved to Florida a few months later, but she tried to keep in touch with Doris. Not long after their last telephone conversation, Nancie heard the dreaded news: Edward had killed Doris. As bizarre as it sounds, this Christian woman was murdered by her own husband, a deacon in a Pentecostal church. Those who counsel abused women say this story is not as unique as it sounds.

As is often the case, this church's pastor doubted the battered woman's story, so he dragged his feet instead of properly dealing with a life-and-death situation. He shrugged off this report of a Christian man who acted in a domineering manner—since authoritarian behavior in the home is actually encouraged by many pastors.

After all, if a man erupts in anger at home or is overly demanding, isn't he just demonstrating that he is in charge? Isn't it a godly virtue for Christian men to act strong and authoritarian? Isn't it true that if a man doesn't remain in absolute control, he is in danger of becoming spiritually weak, and this is opening up a door for spiritual attack on his home? Many evangelical Christian men today might agree with this philosophy—but the logic is ridiculous. We should also note that Paul told Timothy that a man given to anger is not qualified to serve in ministry. (See 1 Timothy 3:3.)

One of the most comprehensive studies on domestic violence in the church was conducted in the mid-1980s by clinical psychologist Jim M. Alsdurf, a graduate of Fuller Theological Seminary. Based on a questionnaire sent to fifty-seven hundred Protestant pastors in the United States and Canada, the survey revealed that though most pastors regularly confront spouse abuse in their ministries, they often are not overly concerned because they view the situation from a patriarchal perspective. In essence, this attitude says, "According to the Bible, Christian men are supposed to be in charge of the home, so a little yelling and hitting is OK." Consider Alsdurf's findings:

- Twenty-six percent of the pastors polled said they normally tell a woman who is being abused by her husband that she should continue to submit to him "and to trust that God would honor her action by either stopping the abuse or giving her the strength to endure it."

- About 25 percent of the respondents said a lack of submissiveness in the wife is what triggered the violence in the first place. In other words, these pastors believe that the abuse is actually the woman's fault. The women are told that if they would "learn to submit," the violence will stop.

- A majority of the pastors said it is better for a woman to tolerate some level of violence in the home—even though it is "not God's perfect will"—than to seek separation that might end in divorce. (Is it "better" even if the woman is killed, maimed or raped?)

- Seventy-one percent of the ministers said they would never advise a battered wife to leave her husband or separate because of abuse, and 92 percent said they would never counsel her to seek divorce.[5]

Christian homes and churches are in a sad state indeed if there have not been significant changes in clergy attitudes since this survey was taken. The Bible is clear on the point that God opposes violence (Prov. 21:7; Ezek. 45:9). In fact, Jesus warned against those who take advantage of people who are physically weaker. Yet we are actually promoting a theology that encourages violence when we tell a woman she must learn to "endure" beatings. (See Matthew 18:1–6.)

A pastor should be willing to counsel a woman to seek separation or divorce when her marriage is jeopardized by domestic violence. Why don't we do this? Because our unbalanced interpretation of Scripture can hinder us from seeing divorce as a viable option for Christians. In a fallen world, however, we must recognize that sometimes it is the only option.

Divorce is a tragic problem in our society, and we can't minimize its negative effects, particularly on children. But some of the Christian community's opposition to divorce has been more of a concern for the church's image than for the individuals involved. We aren't proud of the fact that so many Christian marriages fail, so we don't want to do anything to make the statistics worse.

James and Phyllis Alsdurf point out in their book *Abuse and Religion* that we evangelicals are fond of quoting Malachi 2:16, "For the LORD God of Israel says that He hates divorce" (NKJV). Yet if we go to the next sentence we read, "And I hate a man's covering himself with violence as well as with his garment" (NIV). A footnote in the New International Version says the verse can be translated, "I hate a man's covering his wife with violence."[6]

Yes, God hates divorce. But we can see in this passage in Malachi that He also hates wife-beating and any other form of abuse. Women do not have to stay in dangerous marital situations just to keep divorce statistics low. God cares deeply about the safety and well-being of women. He is not concerned that one more divorce will mar the church's image. We too need to start caring more about vulnerable women (and their children) than about how another divorce might look on our record.

Irresponsible Theology

A distraught Christian woman who had been regularly beaten by her husband for four years finally gained the courage to seek counsel from her pastor, who was affiliated with a prominent evangelical denomination. She told him about her husband's addiction to pornography, his fits of rage and how he had once thrown her against a wall so hard that she heard a cracking sound in the back of her neck.

The pastor's response was frightening: "If your husband kills you," he advised, "it will be to the glory of God." Her only option, he told her, was to submit and pray that God would change her husband's heart.

This is perverted! How did we ever invent a "Christian" theology that encourages a woman to risk injury or death at the hands of her husband to please God? How warped a woman's view of God would have to be for her to accept such counsel!

The root problem with our theology is that the church has taught that men have a biblical right to dominate—and we have instructed women that their submission to this ungodly behavior is God-ordained suffering, which they must willingly bear. This butchering of biblical texts distorts the character of Christ—who spent much of His time teaching on God's care for the oppressed.

Let's look carefully at a verse that is most often used to promote this wrong view, and set the record straight.

Because the apostle Paul told women to "submit to your husbands as to the Lord" (Eph. 5:22, NIV), we have assumed that women should have no say in family matters or that their opinion is second-rate. This verse, taken out of context, has been twisted to mean that the husband is the boss and that the woman must obey his every whim. We portray marriage as a hierarchy, with husbands on the throne and wives at the footstool.

But this is not a Christian view of marriage at all. The first rule of biblical hermeneutics is that we look at *all of Scripture* to clarify the meaning of a particular text. So before we can understand this one verse, we must look at what the Bible in general teaches about submission and authority.

In more than one instance Jesus taught that a true leader in the kingdom of God is a *servant*. He said the greatest must be the *least*. He told His disciples that they must become as *children*. He said in Mark 10:44 that "whoever wishes to be first among you shall be *slave of all*" (emphasis added.)

How do we apply this passage to marriage? Certainly it should be clear that if a man is called to lead a family, his leadership must be Christlike. He must serve, not dictate. He must display humility, not a know-it-all attitude. He must lead from a position of meekness, not from prideful superiority or tyrannical domination.

In fact, Jesus flatly condemned the worldly style of top-down, hierarchical leadership when He taught that His kingdom is not like that of the Gentiles, whose leaders "lord it over" their subordinates. (See Matthew 20:25–26.) Why would Christ condemn this kind of behavior on one hand and then encourage husbands to act in an authoritarian manner at home? He didn't, and neither did the apostle Paul.

When we read Paul's discourse on marriage in Ephesians 5, we must start with verse 21, "Submit *to one another* out of reverence for Christ" (NIV, emphasis added). This verse has been conveniently overlooked in many Christian marriage seminars, which usually start the lesson with verse 22, "Wives, submit to your husbands" (NIV). I have often heard teachings on the subject of male headship in the home, but I've never heard a pastor encourage men to submit to their wives as suggested in verse 21. Yet in a loving marriage, a man and woman will defer to one another when they make decisions.

A closer look at this passage reveals that this teaching begins with verse 21, which encourages all believers to submit to one another "in the fear of the Christ." To promote an attitude of submissiveness in the entire church, Paul tells wives to submit to their husbands, husbands to their wives, children to their parents and slaves to their masters. Submission, not in the sense of domination or rulership over another, but in the sense of preferring one another and not demanding personal rights, should be operating in the entire body of Christ in order to reveal the love of Christ to the world.

We also must note that the Greek word for submission, *hupotasso,* is written in the Greek middle voice, which means it is something that an individual imposes upon himself or herself. It means to choose to yield to another, rather than demanding one's own way. Submission remains the freewill right of the one choosing to yield. *It cannot be demanded from another individual or imposed upon one person by another.* When this occurs, it stops being *hupotasso* and becomes *domination,* which was an attitude Christ forbade His disciples to operate in with regard to one another (Matt. 23:10). Submission is not something that can be required or exacted from another person.

The overarching theme of marriage in the Bible is the concept of *unity* and *oneness.* Couples should develop a deep level of intimacy and trust that blossoms as they work out differences, share dreams and walk through hardships together. In my sixteen years of marriage, my wife and I have had plenty of disagreements: over finances, over the education of our children and over trivial matters. But when we disagree, I do not announce, "I am the head of this house, so what I say goes." When we reach an impasse, Deborah and I either agree to pray for a season about the matter, or we choose to defer to one another. This is the concept of biblical submission that the apostle Paul attempted to convey in Ephesians. I don't demand my way, and Deborah doesn't demand hers. Instead, we both humbly seek after God's way, His will and His purpose. When our hearts are truly His, biblical submission is easy.

The point is never who is right or wrong or who is in charge. The issue is how we can discover the mind of Christ. I view my wife as an equal. I am not "over her." We function as one.

Paul told husbands, "This is how you love your wives, by giving up your life, your way and your rights, as Christ gave up His." Remember that Christ was Lord of the universe and laid down His crown by submitting Himself unto death. The Bible says He took on the form of a servant. He laid down His life to raise us up. This is the purpose of biblical submission.

We must notice also in studying Ephesians 5 that Paul does not focus the text solely on the need for wifely submission. His words in this passage stress the loving attitude husbands should demonstrate at home. Men are commanded to love their wives "as Christ also loved the church" (v. 25) and "as their own bodies" (v. 28). These words were revolutionary in a first-century culture that taught that wives were their husband's property!

Marriages are doomed to serious dysfunction and ultimate failure if the husband views his wife as inferior or if he arrogantly assumes that God wants him to always have the right answer and the wisest plan in every situation. No! The reason God provided Adam with Eve was because the man couldn't do it alone. He needed an equal partner who complemented him in every way.

So, Is the Husband the Boss?

The passage of Scripture that is so often misused with regard to the complex issue of male headship is Ephesians 5:22–23:

Wives, be subject to your own husbands, as to the Lord. For the husband is the *head* of the wife, as Christ also is the head of the church.

—EMPHASIS ADDED

Contrary to popular interpretation, these verses do not give men a license to dominate their wives, nor do they endorse a kind of top-down hierarchy in the marriage relationship.

One of Paul's main reasons for writing this discourse on family relationships was to stress the beauty of the mystical union between man and wife, which he compares to the communion between Christ and the church. If Paul were trying to declare who was in charge, he would have said, "Wives, *obey* your husbands," in the same manner that he states in Colossians 3:20, "Children, *obey* your parents" (NIV). But he does not use the word *obey*.

The word *hupotasso* can also mean "to identify with" or "to be attached to." It can also mean "become one with." Again, the issue here is oneness and unity between equal partners, not who obeys whom.

But there is another important reason Paul wrote these words, and we cannot understand their meaning without delving deeper into the culture of the New Testament period. Theologian Catherine Clark Kroeger has noted that in the first century, women had no rights and were considered possessions. In the Roman Empire, it was customary for the woman's father to continue to claim ownership of his daughter even after she was married.

This inhumane system, known as *sine manu*, or "marriage without hand," was a way for the bride's dowry to stay under the control of her father even after she moved into her husband's home. As long as she was brought back to her father's house three times a year (sometimes against her will), he could claim legal ownership of her and her property. This system, which was later outlawed, obviously created havoc in families. [7]

Knowing the context helps us understand why Paul stressed to the new Christian community in Ephesus that a wife should "be attached to" or "submitted to" or "identified with" her husband. She was no longer to be attached to her father! And this is why

Paul, a few verses later, quotes Genesis 2:24: "For this reason a man shall leave his father and mother and be joined to his wife, and the two shall become one flesh" (Eph. 5:31, NKJV).

But if this passage in Ephesians does not give men permission to dominate their wives, then why does Paul say that a husband is "head" (5:23) of the wife?

The Greek word for "head" in this passage is *kephale*, which is most often translated "authority over." However, some Bible scholars point out that this word can and often is translated "source" in ancient texts, in much the same way that we would refer to the "head" of a river being its source. Therefore it is possible that *kephale* can mean here that man is the *source* of woman, a reference to the fact that Eve was created from Adam.

Again, many scholars believe that Paul is setting in order the true Christian family in the midst of a pagan Roman culture that treated women like property and disregarded the autonomy of a newlywed couple. According to God's plan, when a man and a woman come together in holy matrimony they must sever their ties to parents, grandparents and any other controlling influences from relatives. The man must leave his father and mother and cleave to his wife. (See Genesis 2:24; Ephesians 5:31.) She must "submit," or "become attached to," her husband, rather than continue to relate to her father as her "head."

If we truly want to understand the meaning of Ephesians 5, these cultural factors must be considered. Paul's words to this infant New Testament church were meant to liberate women who had been subjected to a patriarchal system that did not even recognize their personhood. The gospel proclaimed in this passage set in motion a way to revolutionize that culture—and to transform the nature of men who did not know how to love their wives.

How tragic that we have used Paul's liberating words to put women in bondage!

Gender Bias Around the World

Gender prejudice has been at the core of fallen human nature since the Garden of Eden, and we see its effects everywhere. It is the way of the world. It has been encoded in all of the world's religions. A degrading view of women is pervasive in almost every culture, but nowhere is it more evident than in the Middle East.

The stories of abuse of women from the Muslim world are horrific. Take for example the case of a Palestinian girl named Saana, who at age eighteen was forced into an arranged marriage to a Muslim man she didn't love. *The Middle East Intelligence Digest* reported her tragic story to illustrate that women are incredibly vulnerable in a culture that considers females to be the literal property of their husbands or other male relatives.

Because Saana was so unhappy, she ran away from her new home at one point and ended up with friends in another West Bank village. Her family tracked her down within six hours and forced her to return to her husband. The next day, Saana's brother killed her, decapitated her body and carried her severed head through the streets. His act of brutality, which was praised by the local Muslim townsfolk, is what is known in that region as a "family honor killing." Because Saana had "disgraced" her husband by running away, she got what she deserved according to Islamic tradition.[8]

At least forty such murders are reported in Israel's Palestinian territories each year, although the number of actual honor killings is probably much higher. In 1994, one woman was seized in broad daylight in east Jerusalem and stabbed sixteen times in the head and shoulder. Her crime: She had insisted on custody of her children in a complicated divorce case.

In a report released in 2000 by Amnesty International and the United Nations, researchers said as many as one thousand Muslim "honor killings" occurred in Pakistan in 1999. At least four hundred such killings were documented in Yemen in 1997. In a majority of the cases, the UN found that the orders to kill the women came from family members.[9]

The Associated Press reported in July 2000 that the father of one twenty-eight-year-old Pakistani woman who had "disgraced" her family by seeking a divorce from her abusive husband hired an assassin to shoot her. Her father, a prominent businessman in the city of Lahore, was praised by religious and community leaders for killing his daughter.[10]

In Iran, Afghanistan and Saudi Arabia, and in other Muslim nations where Western influence is strongly resisted, the human rights of women are extremely limited because of Islamic teachings. Women in some Muslim cultures are often strongly discouraged from pursuing any kind of education, and they are considered to be on the same social level as domesticated animals. Muslim women in these Arab nations have been shot, beheaded, stoned or poisoned for "crimes" such as sitting next to a man on a bus, talking to a man on the telephone or being raped.

Some Muslim women don't even have the right to venture out in public. Abassi Madani, leader of the Algerian Islamic Front, was recently asked by *Time* magazine when it was appropriate for a Muslim woman to leave her house. His response: "When she is born, when she is married and when she goes to the cemetery."[11]

Fundamentalist Islam endorses spouse abuse in its cruelest form. Consider what the Qur'an and other holy Muslim texts, or Hadiths, say about marriage and Allah's will for women:

- Men are superior to women (Q 2:228, Q 4:34).

- Women are deficient in intelligence, gratitude and religion (Hadith *Sahih al-Bukhari*) and are to be considered "toys" (Hadith No. 919).

- The deception of women is "awesome," their wickedness is contagious, and bad character and feeble minds are their predominant traits (Hadith *Ihy'a 'Uloum ed-Din*).

- The witness of two women is equal to the witness of one man (Q 2:282).

- Women must wear veils, or *hijabs,* to protect not their own chastity but the chastity of men who might see them (Hadith by Dr. Mohammad Sa'id Ramadan al-Buti).

- A husband's rights over his wife are divine (Hadith *Mishkat al-Masabih*).

- It is condescension on the part of the man to spend his life with a woman. She cannot repay this favor, no matter what sacrifice she makes (Hadith by Suyuti).

- A husband who fears rebelliousness in his wife must admonish her first. If that does not work, he has the right to desert her sexually. If that does not work, he may beat her (Q 4:34).

- A footnote in the English translation of the Hadith Mishkat al-Masabih states that a husband may beat his wife mildly if she (1) does not wear "fineries" that he requests, (2) refuses sexual relations without a lawful excuse, (3) is ordered to take a bath to clean herself from impurities for prayer, and refuses, and (4) goes abroad without permission of her husband.

- The Muslim cleric Ibn Kaathir, commenting on a Qu'ranic passage in Q 4:34, says that a man is not to be asked why he beat his wife. It is his unquestionable right.

- Beatings will not only reform "deviations" in behavior but can also be gratifying to women. Some women will not "recognize the power of the man whom they love except when the man conquers them physically" (Sayid Qotb, *Fi Zilal al-Qur'an*, commenting on Q 4:34).[12]

Islam isn't the only religion that still promotes wife-beating and female subjugation in the twenty-first century. Hinduism, which boasts an estimated 714 million adherents in India alone, also promotes a degrading view of women even though some of its most important deities are powerful goddesses.

Because of the rise of militant religious nationalism, many Hindus in India today still practice barbaric rituals such as *sati*, the ancient tradition of burning women on funeral pyres after their husbands die. Also in many parts of India today, female babies often are killed quietly by their parents because it is considered shameful to give birth to a girl. The United Nations recently reported that up to fifty million girls are missing from India's population because of infanticide.[13]

Shouldn't Christianity Be Different?

Compared to the abysmal record of human rights abuses evident in Muslim and Hindu cultures, one would expect the status of women to be higher in nations that have been influenced by the gospel. In most cases this is true—it was the influence of Christianity in the United States, for example, that sparked the movement to give women the vote in 1920.

Similar movements occurred later in Canada (1918), Germany (1918), Sweden (1921), France (1944) and Italy (1945). England granted the vote to women in 1918 but required them to be age thirty, while men could vote at age twenty-one; the voting age was not equalized until 1928. Iraq waited until 1980 to grant women's suffrage. South African black women could not vote until 1994.[14]

Governments have finally recognized that women deserve equal rights, yet in the church the degradation of women through spouse abuse still occurs in the Christian church to an embarrassing extent. Although part of Jesus Christ's mission was to redeem women from the curse and to elevate them to a place of safety and righteous influence, church leaders have not always supported that mission. In many cases we have opposed it.

In New Testament times, women were considered the absolute property of their fathers or husbands. They were less valuable than cattle. This is why the apostle Paul's words to husbands in Ephesians 5:28, "Husbands ought also to love their own wives as their own bodies," was such a radical departure from the cultural traditions of the day. The Christian view of husband-wife relationships is one of *equality* and *mutual respect*, not domination, control and humiliation.

Yet gender prejudice remained entrenched in the church in its earliest days. Throughout the Middle Ages the predominant view among Christians was that women were inferior and should be ruled by their tyrant husbands—and beaten if necessary. Catholic clergy in medieval times endorsed wife-beating for the purpose of discipline, and this was law in France in the thirteenth century. One law stated that men "may be excused for the injuries they inflict on their wives. Provided he neither kills nor maims her, it is legal for a man to beat his wife if she wrongs him."[15]

Although the Protestant Reformation brought a new understanding of the grace of God for salvation, the chief reformers offered little of that grace to women. John Calvin, John Knox and Martin Luther all displayed blatant chauvinism in their writings, and Luther actually boasted that he hit his wife to correct her.[16]

In Protestant England, wife-beating was a protected act as long as the instrument used was not considered "unreasonable." (One law specified that the stick used to strike a woman could not be thicker than a man's thumb, and some etymologists claim that this evolved into our modern figure of speech, "rule of thumb.") In the United States, lawmakers finally began enacting statutes in the late 1800s that made wife-beating a punishable crime.

Women in the twentieth century gained political rights and equal access in the workplace, yet today spouse abuse is still a wide-spread problem. The National Council on Domestic Violence says a woman is battered every fifteen seconds in this country.[17] Tragically, the problem also exists in evangelical churches—but it is often swept under a rug because Christian leaders either don't know how to stop it or can't reconcile the problem with their theology. That's because their own teaching about marriage relation-ships, particularly their philosophy of wives and "biblical submission," is an underlying cause of this ugly dilemma.

Isn't it time that the church stood up and shined a truly biblical light of truth into the world's dark history of gender bias?

Chapter 10
Questions for Discussion

1. How would you counsel a woman whose Christian husband is abusing her physically?

2. Explain how you interpret the apostle Paul's words in Ephesians 5:22, "Wives submit to your husbands" (NIV).

3. After reading the quotes from Islamic holy books, how would you describe the Muslim view of women? How does this view differ from a Christian view of women?

4. Explain why you think Christians in other time periods actually promoted the practice of wife-beating.

The prophet Joel was not against the daughters prophesying, nor the apostles… So you that persecute the daughters on whom the Spirit of the Lord is poured, and believe them not, you are them that despise prophesying, and so have broken the apostles' command.… So be ashamed forever, and let all your mouths be stopped forever, that despise the spirit of prophecy in the daughters, and do cast them into prison, and do hinder the women laborers in the gospel.[1]

—GEORGE FOX, FOUNDER OF THE QUAKER MOVEMENT

Oh, that the ministers of religion would search the original records of God's Word in order to discover whether the general notions of society are not wrong on this subject, and whether God really intended woman to bury her gifts and talents, as she now does.[2]

—CATHERINE BOOTH, CO-FOUNDER OF THE SALVATION ARMY

It is not enough for women to modestly and quietly seek their own redemption; they must proclaim it, even when that proclamation lays them open to the false charge of immodesty. It is wicked for any human being to shut the mouth of anyone, male or female, who will sound forth a testimony to the truth in these days of apostasy.[3]

—MISSIONARY AND BIBLE EXPOSITOR KATHERINE BUSHNELL, WHO HELPED STOP CHILD PROSTITUTION IN INDIA IN THE LATE 1800S

Between four and five years after my sanctification, on a certain time, an impressive silence fell upon me, and I stood as if someone was about to speak to me, yet I had no such thought in my heart. But to my utter surprise there seemed to sound a voice which I thought I distinctly heard, and most certainly understood, which said to me "Go preach the gospel!" I immediately replied aloud, "No one will believe me." Again I listened, and again the same voice seemed to say— "Preach the gospel. I will put words in your mouth."[4]

—JERENA LEE, THE FIRST WIDELY TRAVELED FEMALE EVANGELIST IN THE AFRICAN METHODIST EPISCOPAL CHURCH DURING THE EARLY 1800S

10 Lies

CONCLUSION

Hundreds of American pastors flocked to South Korea during the 1970s and '80s to observe the remarkable ministry of Dr. David Yonggi Cho, founder of the world's largest church. At that time his Pentecostal congregation in the city of Seoul had already mushroomed to two hundred thousand members—in a nation where Christianity had only been allowed to be legally tolerated for one century. Americans wanted to know Dr. Cho's secret so they could duplicate his incredible church-growth success.

When the Americans returned from Korea, they announced to the evangelical establishment that Cho's secret was twofold: (1) He relied heavily on prayer and motivated his congregation to pray for hours each week; and (2) he divided his congregation into small "cell groups" that met in homes, giving converts the proper outlet for regular discipleship. So in typical American fashion, churches in the United States adopted prayer programs and experimented with Cho's cell-group model. The goal was to build American churches as big as Cho's Yoido Full Gospel congregation.

But so far, the largest churches in the United States have barely broken the twenty-thousand-member threshold, while Cho's congregation had hit seven hundred thousand by the year 2000. Obviously we missed something in the translation when we tried to copy the Korean formula.

While prayer certainly was a key ingredient in the spreading of the gospel in Seoul, Cho revealed in 1999 during a message to pastors and missionaries in Italy that experts had overlooked a major factor in the growth of Yoido Full Gospel Church. He then went on to inform them about the key role women have played in his ministry:

> For five thousand years in Korea women had no voice at all. They were only to cater to the needs of men. Then Christianity came and set women free. Especially in the church, women are free in Korea. In ministry they are equal with men. They are licensed. They are ordained. And they become the cell leaders. Out of fifty thousand cell leaders in my church, forty-seven thousand are women. I have about six hundred associate pastors. Four hundred of them are women. They are wonderful workers. Without women I don't think I could have built up this big church.
>
> I am not the only one who uses women. The Presbyterians, Methodists, Holiness and Baptists all use women. But this is not what you do in Italy. You don't use women. They come and warm the bench. If you ever train the women, and delegate your ministry to them, they will become tremendous messengers for the Lord.
>
> Some of you are going to quote 1 Corinthians 14:34, "Women are to be silent in the church." I'll tell you one thing, brothers and sisters. Once women are called into the ministry, they no longer belong to the category of women. They are messengers of the Lord.
>
> So, I'm not afraid of having women workers. Because by empowering women we are evangelizing all of Korea. I'm encouraging American churches to use women. European pastors are very slow to learn this. I come and encourage them to use women.[5]

Cho told the Italians that he almost suffered a nervous break-down in 1964 when he began his ministry because he was attempting to do all the work himself. During a period of exhaustion, under a doctor's care, he realized that the New Testament church was led by pastors who opened their homes for fellowship and teaching. Cho also recognized from studying the Scriptures that the apostle Paul placed first-century women such as Priscilla and Lydia in pastoral roles to operate house churches. So Cho began training a large group of female cell-church leaders, and in response, many of his trusted male leaders got angry and left the church.

Cho was physically unable to return to the pastorate until 1969 due to the effects of stress. But during those five years, when these women led his congregation in small groups, Yoido Full Gospel grew from three thousand to eighteen thousand members—a 43 percent annual growth rate.

What if American Christians who visited Seoul had duplicated Cho's strategy by empowering women to serve in every available church role? Doubtless, some men would have left their churches in disgust—announcing how "unbiblical" it is to employ women to lead church services or exercise spiritual authority over men. But perhaps if we had allowed women to serve, rather than keeping them tied up like donkeys in a stall, American churches would have grown instead of having shrunk since the 1980s. And per-haps by now we would have a congregation in the United States with seven hundred thousand members.

Women in the Harvest Fields

Church leaders in other parts of the world have employed Cho's secret weapon. Rather than expecting women to sit passively in the shadows while men do all the work of ministry, they have brought women to the forefront in the mission fields of Africa, Asia and the Middle East. These women are serving as doctors, pastors, teachers and relief workers. Some have established orphanages for slum dwellers or launched rescue efforts to pull children out of slavery or prostitution. Others are teaching in seminaries and Bible colleges. Some are risking their lives to preach in nations where it is illegal to openly share the gospel. A few are leading entire denominations.

A report released in the year 2000 by the U.S.-based organization Discipling a Whole Nation (DAWN) said that many of the existing Christian churches in one Muslim nation have been started by women.[6] This is also happening in places such as the Philippines and Cambodia. And in China, American missionaries who have visited the thriving unregistered "house churches" there say a majority of full-time itinerant evangelists are female. Some observers estimate that women make up 85 percent of the Chinese church's underground leadership. They are serving a revival movement that has grown from 1.8 million Protestants in 1949 to as many as 75 million today.[7]

Dr. Cho's secret weapon is not a new concept. Women have been used by the Holy Spirit to preach the gospel since Jesus Christ commissioned the Samaritan woman to tell her neighbors about the Messiah. But women ministers have always faced opposition from within the church because of chauvinism and ingrained cultural prejudice.

During the 1800s, when huge numbers of women sailed to India, China and Africa to serve as teachers, translators and evangelists, they became a threat to male leadership in the mission stations because of their sheer numbers. The women were often reminded who was in charge, but most of them remained meek and compliant in the face of discrimination. They were content to do all the work and take none of the credit.

One missionary who challenged the chauvinists of her day was Southern Baptist pioneer Lottie Moon. During her stay in China during the 1870s, she complained loudly to her superiors about the way female ministers were pushed to the side. "What women want who come to China," she said, "is free opportunity to do the largest possible work. What women have a right to demand is perfect equality."[8]

Yet more than one hundred twenty years after Lottie Moon wrote these words, the denomination she served until her death is still denying women the opportunity to serve in all ministry capacities. As stated earlier, the Southern Baptist Convention reiterated its anti-women position during its annual meeting in Orlando,

Florida, in 2000, claiming that the Bible prohibits women from being senior pastors.

How many more years will we drag our feet and be content with meager results when God is offering supernatural breakthroughs such as what Dr. Cho has seen in Korea? How many millions of people will slip into hell because we wouldn't let women do their part to reach them?

For the sake of this great harvest we must set the women free to preach and to lead. We cannot postpone this. We cannot afford to appoint committees to study the issue of women in ministry any longer. We cannot allow culture and human prejudice to control us. Men cannot be threatened by women who simply want to obey God.

I suggest we take these ten important steps to fully empower women for church leadership:

1. We must repent and apologize for gender prejudice.

Our record of wrongs is too lengthy to list. From the very beginning of the Christian era, we have allowed cultural prejudice against women to prevail in God's house. Pastors in the Middle Ages used the Bible to defend wife beating. During the Inquisition period, both Catholic and Protestant leaders falsely accused women of witchcraft, denying them fair trials, and then they tortured them, burned them at the stake or drowned them. Later, Christians resisted efforts to grant women the right to own property, leaving them destitute if they were abandoned by divorce or the death of their husbands.

During the 1800s, church leaders opposed allowing women to pursue higher education. Some pastors even promoted the view that women were physiologically and mentally inferior—and therefore were not qualified to attend college or medical school. Church leaders in the United States also vehemently opposed giving women the right to vote, even though the earliest leaders of the women's suffrage movement were Bible-believing Christians. And even today, many denominational leaders oppose giving women the opportunity to pastor churches or serve in other top ministry positions.

We have so much to repent for. Male pride is at the root of our sin. A domineering patriarchal attitude has brought about sexual abuse, domestic violence, pornography, adultery and rampant divorce, often sending women into prisons of depression, eating disorders, addiction and even lesbianism. (Many women who struggle with homosexuality admit they were molested by a male relative, and they say the shame of the experience caused them to hate men.)

We must pursue reconciliation, but it can occur only with heart-felt repentance and sincere apologies. Husbands must apologize to wives. Pastors must apologize to their female church members. Ministry leaders must ask forgiveness from female employees who have been denied opportunities and financial rewards. And denominations must issue public statements of repentance for gender prejudice.

In 1996, leaders of the International Pentecostal Holiness Church convened in Fayetteville, North Carolina, for a "solemn assembly" in which they repented publicly for corporate sins they felt had grieved God and impeded their progress as a movement. One of those sins was male domination. A statement they read on August 23, 1996, said, in part:

> We, the men of the Pentecostal Holiness Church, confess that we have not honored the precedent set forth in God's Word. Often, we have not treated our wives as equal partners in marriage and ministry. We have distorted the doctrine of holiness by focusing on the external appearance of women. We recognize the sin of male domination and acknowledge that we have withheld from women places of honor in the church. We have not affirmed the ministries of qualified women by releasing them to serve in places of leadership. We have shown inequity regarding their wages.
>
> Forgive us, O Father, of the sin of male domination which has made our spouses feel like unequal partners. We repent of our unbiblical treatment of women with regard to their ministries and wages. We repent of targeting them in our teaching on holiness and of abusing them verbally, both in public and in private.

Create in us a new sensitivity to the God-given gifts of the women in the International Pentecostal Holiness Church, that there may be unity and greater power in our worldwide ministry.[9]

Every denomination in the United States would do well to follow the Pentecostal Holiness example.

2. Christian men must vocally defend the right of women to preach the gospel and lead the church.

When I became passionate about releasing women into ministry a few years ago, some people began to ask me why I, as a man, had taken up this cause. Some accused me of being a feminist. Others quietly wondered how I could be secure in my manhood and at the same time read books by female theologians—as if studying their writings might weaken my masculinity.

I am passionate about the issue of women in ministry because it is a concern on the heart of God. This is high on His agenda. The Father wants to release His daughters!

Throughout history, whenever women have been empowered as missionaries, evangelists and church planters, brave men were always willing to side with God on this issue—even though a majority of men in the church's proverbial "good old boys club" stood firmly in their chauvinism. Those of us who favor empowering women are in good company:

- George Fox, founder of the Society of Friends (the Quakers), released a small army of anointed women preachers in early colonial America. He quoted the prophecy of Joel 2:28, "Your daughters shall prophesy," as his biblical defense.

- Revivalist Jonathan Edwards upset the religious carts of his day when he publicly encouraged women to testify of their faith.

- John Wesley, the founder of Methodism, initially opposed women in ministry, but later changed his position and was criticized because so many of his female colleagues preached openly and led revivals.

- Charles G. Finney, leader of the Second Great Awakening in the United States, never supported the right of women to hold office in the church, but he was denounced for allowing women to pray and testify in his meetings. He also taught that "the church that silences the women is shorn of half its power."

- William Booth, who founded the Salvation Army with his wife, Catherine, shared preaching duties with her. During one period in the 1860s, he preached on Sundays on the east side of London while Catherine preached on the west side. His ministry officially outlawed discrimination against females in 1875, and in three years almost half of Salvation Army officers were women. Thus the reason for Booth's famous quote, "Some of my best men are women."[10]

- In the mid-1800s, a wave of female missionaries headed toward Asia and Africa from the United States. The men who sent them recognized that they had been mobilized by the hand of God. Although sex discrimination was rampant on the mission field and women were often reminded of their "proper place," missionary statesmen, including Hudson Taylor of the China Inland Mission and C. T. Studd of the Worldwide Evangelization Crusade, vigorously defended the spiritual accomplishments of their female workers.

It is time for men to stand on the right side of this issue. If the Lord of the harvest is sending our sisters, who are we to stand in their way?

3. The church must stop misusing the Scriptures to limit the ministry of women.

The gospel is good news for women. Yet for centuries the church has insisted that the curse of subjection and degradation placed on Eve must forever remain on all women, even though Christ redeemed them from the curse. Even in the twenty-first century, churches still teach that it is God's will for women to remain in a perpetual second-class status. Though Jesus preached liberty to the captives, we have preached bondage.

Fallen men have imposed their own gender biases upon the Bible, and this action has resulted in gross mistranslation and mis-interpretation. Men have read their prejudices into the Scriptures and then codified these views as sacred religious precepts—when in fact they run totally contrary to the heart of the gospel. We say women can't preach, when in fact the Bible commands women to be Christ's bold witnesses. We say women can't prophesy, when the prophet Joel declared that they would, and the apostle Paul gave specific instructions on how they should. We say women can't lead the church when, in fact, the Bible gives numerous examples of godly women leaders.

We are like the Pharisees, smug in our enlightened under-standing of the Scriptures. They were the keepers of the law, but they became so entrenched in their own interpretations of the Bible that they didn't recognize the incarnate Word of God when He stood in their midst.

When Jesus visited the temple on the Sabbath and healed a woman who had been bent over for eighteen years, they dis-missed the miracle and indignantly accused Jesus of breaking the Sabbath. (See Luke 13:10−17.) These men were so locked into their religious traditions that they could not recognize the hand of God at work right in front of their eyes. And they quoted the Bible to defend their opposition to Him.

We desperately need to be delivered from the spirit of the Pharisees. Countless women today, like the woman in Luke 13, have been healed by the Savior and are eager to tell multitudes about His love and power. Jesus did not tell the crippled woman to shut up, yet we insist on silencing women who are called to preach—and we are quick to quote scriptures out of context to justify our position.

4. Bible-believing churches must dismiss the notion that women's ordination is a "liberal" position.

Conservative denominations in recent years have demonized feminism and blamed all our society's ills on the feminist move-ment. Some Christians actually believe that the breakdown of the family and the erosion of all moral values is the fault of women who demanded equal rights in the workplace.

But we must make the distinction between secular feminism and *biblical feminism,* which has its roots in Scripture. In her excellent book *Equal to Serve,* author Gretchen Gaebelein Hull makes this point clear:

> The secular feminist says: "I want my rights. I want to be able to compete on an equal basis with men." The biblical feminist says: "I want to be free to be the person God created me to be and to have the privilege of following Christ as He calls me to do."
>
> Feminism (or any other *ism*) without Christ is just another power struggle. But adding the word *biblical* to feminism indicates that these feminists want to explore their conviction about equality of women in a biblical way and implement their findings according to biblical guidelines.[11]

We don't have to be afraid of biblical feminism. If the Bible champions the idea that women are equal with men in the eyes of God and that they should be treated with fairness and respect, then this must become part of the gospel we preach.

Many mainline denominations, including the Episcopal Church, the United Methodist Church and the Disciples of Christ, began sliding into a tragic theological crisis during the 1950s and '60s. Leading bishops and seminarians questioned basic Christian precepts such as the virgin birth and the divine inspiration of Scripture. At the same time, these groups began discussing whether Christian moral positions on abortion and homosexuality should be reexamined. As God's Word was compromised for the sake of political correctness, these churches also gave the secular feminist movement a place to thrive.

In response, many other churches, including conservative evangelical churches, became the self-declared enemies of the mainline denominations. The battle lines were drawn, and the struggle became one of "us vs. them." Conservatives opposed gay marriage; liberals supported it. Conservatives opposed abortion; liberals favored it. When the mainline denominations began ordaining women, conservative denominations viewed this as additional evidence of apostasy.

But women's ordination is not a liberal position. We cannot call evil what God has said is good. Many of the great revivalists throughout the history of Christianity believed that God calls Spirit-empowered women to preach and serve the church in leadership positions. And every time in history when an outpouring of revival has occurred, women have always assumed a prominent place as carriers of God's holy fire. These women preachers from previous revival periods were certainly not theological liberals, and they would have raised their voices the loudest to denounce the spiritual adultery that has occurred in some mainline churches today.

5. The church must stop ignoring the ugly sin of domestic abuse.

For too long Christian women have been told from the pulpit and in the counseling room that God requires them to submit to emotional and even physical cruelty in order to demonstrate obedience to Ephesians 5:22, "Wives, submit to your husbands as to the Lord" (NIV). Many women in the church are living in prisons of pain because their Christian husbands are physically abusing them. Some of these women have suffered serious physical harm. A few have died.

The church must put an end to this madness. We must offer women healing and transformation rather than denial and blame. By twisting Ephesians 5 to suggest that God wants women to submit to beatings or rape, we have created an environment in which abuse has permission to thrive. Rather than encouraging women to tolerate domestic violence, we must demand repentance from the men who abuse them.

This means we need a new paradigm for men's ministry. Rather than teaching Christian men how to be "in charge," or how to develop proper "male headship," we must teach them how to treat their wives as their equals. Husbands must learn to follow the Christlike model of servant leadership, which empowers others instead of seeking to control and dominate.

6. Christian women must respond to injustice with forgiveness—not revenge.

Anger has fueled the secular feminist movement. During the early 1970s, militant feminists who campaigned for the passage of an Equal Rights Amendment burned their bras in public and chanted "All men are pigs!" during shocking demonstrations. Their anger was, in many instances, justified because our patriarchal society has been guilty of gross gender discrimination. But the screaming and shouting didn't produce the fruit of righteousness. Revenge is never the answer.

Yes, the church has treated women with unbelievable cruelty. But women who desire to overcome the stronghold of patriarchal pride must do so by trusting in the power of the Holy Spirit—and by exhibiting a Christlike attitude of humility and selfless love. This doesn't mean they should keep their mouths shut, but they must not allow a root of bitterness to poison the message they prophesy to the leaders of the church.

Also, as the doors begin to open to women in ministry, we need to remember that only those women who are called and trained can be elevated to positions of church government. Women who assume positions of authority must demonstrate the character of Jesus—who did not grasp for power but took "the form of a bondservant" (Phil. 2:7). Those individuals whom the church ordains must be called and qualified, regardless of gender. A woman who demands a position of leadership in the church because it is "her right" has missed the point. She is just as guilty of rebellion as the men who resist ordaining trained, anointed women to serve alongside them.

7. The church must reject human control—from male and female—and settle for nothing less than the Holy Spirit's direction.

Many conservative churches vehemently oppose allowing women to serve in positions of leadership because they think God blesses the church only under the leadership of men. How ridiculous! *God does not want His church to be controlled by men or women.* He wants it to be controlled by the Holy Spirit.

Galatians 3:28 says that in Christ "there is neither Jew nor Greek, slave nor free, male nor female" (NIV). In other words, when we are "in Christ," and when the Holy Spirit is operating through human vessels, gender distinctions become irrelevant. God works through human agents, whether men or women, to accomplish His purposes. He doesn't look on the outward appearance; He looks at the heart to see if the image of His Son is evident.

When the prophetess Deborah defeated Israel's enemies in Judges 4, she declared that a woman would be instrumental in winning the final battle (v. 9). This occurred when a maiden named Jael drove a tent spike through the enemy Sisera's head, ending the war and securing forty years of peace for God's people. (See Judges 4:21; 5:31.) God was working through Deborah and Jael—not because they were women, but because they were yielded to His Spirit and understood His purpose. Deborah's prophecy of a female obtaining victory was not intended to glorify women or to create competition between the sexes, but to show that God had performed a miracle that no human could accomplish without His help.

In this hour, the church needs Spirit-empowered men and women who recognize that they are simply vessels for the Master's use. They must be emptied of all selfish ambition. They must decrease so that He can increase. If it is God working through a weak human being, whether male or female, then the glory will go to Him alone—not to human flesh.

8. We must take reconciliation and healing to women who have been offended by the church.

Women have been the backbone of the church despite the fact that they have been denied opportunities to lead it. They have provided the bulk of financial support for most churches as well. In some denominations, such as the African Methodist Episcopal Church, up to 80 percent of the average congregation's members is female.

Yet one recent report by researcher George Barna indicates that a growing number of women are turning away from the church because it has marginalized them. Some of these women are turning to the New Age movement. Some are exploring Wicca, a neo-pagan religion that offers women a sense of empowerment through mystical communion with a nature goddess. Others have simply given up on the institutional church to pursue materialism.

Arkansas-based evangelist Diane Shreve travels thousands of miles every year on a motorcycle to reach hard-core female bikers who have formed their own alternative subculture. They are tough women—often from abusive situations—and most of them assume the church has nothing to offer them. But they are surprised when Diane approaches them with a gospel tract or to start a conversation about Jesus. She has led many of them to Christ.

Diane told *Charisma* magazine in 1999 that her goal is to convince these women that God loves them. "I realize that many of them are in the shape they are in because they don't know what a good daddy is," Diane said. "Therefore I rely on the Holy Spirit to supernaturally reveal the father-heart of God to these 'little girls.'"[12]

We need thousands of Diane Shreves today. We need them to go to the prostitutes and the exploited women who work in topless bars and adult clubs. We need them to share Christ with the intellectuals on our university campuses who laugh at the church because we still preach medieval ideas about women's roles. We need them to minister to the Wiccan priestesses who believe the God of the Bible is an angry, patriarchal deity who hates women. Do we honestly believe that men alone are going to reach all of these wounded people?

9. We need to encourage millions of women to go to the mission field in the twenty-first century.

God is using ordinary women to do extraordinary things today. One of them is Heidi Baker, a seminary-trained American who went to the African nation of Mozambique in 1995 with her husband, Rolland, to manage a dilapidated, government-run orphanage.

Heidi assumed she might spend a few years working with

orphans and perhaps plant a church. But after a dramatic revival experience during a visit to Toronto in 1996, her ministry expanded. By the early part of 2000, the Bakers were overseeing two hundred churches and providing housing, clothes and food for more than six hundred orphans in Mozambique's capital, Maputo. After a disastrous cyclone hit the country, Heidi was called on to provide relief aid for twelve thousand flood victims. About two thousand of them professed Christ during an outreach she organized.[13]

Heidi didn't expect to be used by God in such amazing ways. But during her visit to a conference in Toronto prior to the breakthrough in Maputo, she received prayer for the Holy Spirit's anointing. Heidi felt the power of God so intensely that all she could do during the meeting was lie on the floor. She stayed in this posture for seven days during her visit. Once, after hearing the Lord say to her, "You can do nothing without Me," she saw a vision of Jesus walking through a garbage dump in Mozambique. He was handing poor children royal robes and calling them to His marriage feast.

At that point, Heidi knew that Jesus was calling her to give her life to reach these helpless orphans. Sensing Christ's overwhelming love for them made it easier for her to surrender to the call.

Men cannot fulfill the Great Commission alone—this was never Christ's intention. In fact, when He was describing the way the world would be evangelized, Jesus compared the process to a woman putting leaven in three pecks of meal "until it was all leavened" (Matt. 13:33).

It is interesting that Jesus used a parable involving a woman to describe how the gospel would spread globally from one insignificant city in Israel. I can't help but believe that He was thinking about the vast army of women who would be mobilized in the last days to take His message to the nations. When the job of preaching the gospel to the world is completed, we will discover that women played a major part in the process!

10. Christian women must take an active stance in this crucial hour.

When Esther was made queen of King Ahasuerus' Babylonian

203

kingdom, her cousin Mordecai told her of Haman's sinister plot to destroy all the Jews. Knowing that only Esther could save her people from genocide, he told her:

> For if you remain silent at this time, relief and deliverance will arise for the Jews from another place and you and your father's house will perish. And who knows whether you have not attained royalty for such a time as this?
>
> —ESTHER 4:14

Mordecai commanded his cousin to speak out. Yet today, many men in the church are telling women to be quiet! A world is perishing, and millions will die if they do not hear the gospel of Jesus. Yet we are quibbling over whether it is appropriate for women to break out of their cultural confines and do something bold and daring in order to save lives.

Women of God: You have come into the kingdom for such a time as this. You must intervene. You must intercede. You must speak out. You must obey the call of the Holy Spirit. Don't listen to the religious voices that tell you a virtuous woman spends all her time tending to the mundane matters of hearth and home. Don't listen to those who coax Christian women to focus all their attention on how to be "submissive."

We are in a war! People are perishing! The call of God rests on you, and when you stand before Him on the last day He will not accept lame excuses such as "I was a woman, and they told me to be quiet" or "They told me a man had to do that."

I am certain Esther was tempted to shrink back in the hour of deliverance. She probably had a long list of good excuses. Her culture told her it was inappropriate for a woman to approach the throne so boldly. She could have been executed for daring to speak up. But God didn't excuse her from her assignment.

In this hour God is rallying an army of Esthers who are willing to risk their lives, break patriarchal traditions and contradict society in order to rescue a generation that has been marked for death. Like Esther, you may have to fast and pray for the courage to obey. No matter how inadequate you feel or how afraid you are, you may be called to speak to the highest authorities in the land.

You will have to trust God, and your test of faith may not be easy. Although you may feel miserably helpless, you will be required to lay hold of the courage and faith that is available from the Holy Spirit. He will show Himself mighty on behalf of those who are known as the "weaker sex."

With His mighty power working in you, like the fearless maiden, Jael, in the story of Deborah, you will drive the stake into the head of the enemy.

Conclusion
Questions for Discussion

1. Do you think your church uses women in the same way Dr. David Yonggi Cho has used women to grow Yoido Full Gospel Church in South Korea? If not, what attitudes are preventing your church from empowering women in this way?

2. Read the statement of repentance that the Pentecostal Holiness Church issued in 1996 (on pages 194–195). What emotions does this document produce in you?

3. How do you feel the Bible is misused or misinterpreted in your church to limit the ministry of women?

4. Explain the difference between secular feminism and "biblical feminism."

5. Can you think of women in your life who have been offended by the church? How do you feel you can reach them for Christ?

Notes

Introduction

1. Seth Cook Rees, *The Ideal Pentecostal Church*, (Cincinatti: Knapp, 1897), 41, quoted in Ruth Tucker and Walter Liefeld, *Daughters of the Church: Women and Ministry from New Testament Times to the Present*, (Grand Rapids, MI: Zondervan, 1987), 368.
2. Katherine Bushnell, *God's Word to Women*, (Mossville, IL: God's Word to Women Publishers, n.d.), 316.
3. Frances Willard, *Woman in the Pulpit* (Boston: Lothrop, 1888), 62, quoted in Tucker and Liefeld, *Daughters of the Church*, 274.
4. "Christian Polygamists Cite Support in Bible," Associated Press, *The Orlando Sentinel*, January 22, 2000, E-5.
5. The Dutch Reformed Church of South Africa supported the South African government's policy of *apartheid*, or complete segregation of the races, and its theologians developed an elaborate doctrinal framework to support their idea that God favored the white race. Because of its racist stance, the denomination was excluded from membership in the World Alliance of Reformed Churches in 1982, and the Dutch Reformed view was condemned as a heresy. Finally, in 1989, the church condemned apartheid as sin.
6. Adrienne S. Gaines, "Escape from the KKK," *Charisma*, April 1999, 72.
7. Leigh DeVore, "New Gay Pentecostal Denomination Says Homosexuality Isn't Sinful," *Charisma*, January 2000, 20. On the National Gay Pentecostal Alliance's (NGPA) website, the organization offers a tract, "A Biblical Perspective on Same-Sex Marriage," in which it claims that King David was a homosexual and that he was "married" to Saul's son, Jonathan. The NGPA also twists Scriptures to imply that the Old Testament prophet Daniel was involved in a long-term sexual relationship with the Babylonian eunuch Ashpenaz.

8. Grant L. Martin, *Counseling for Family Violence and Abuse*, (Waco, TX: Word Books), 23.

9. Tucker and Liefeld, *Daughters of the Church*, 284.

10. Rabbi Eliezar, quoted in Mishnah Sotah 3.4; B. Sotah 20a, quoted in Tucker and Liefeld, *Daughters of the Church*, 60.

11. Warren C. Trenchard, *Ben Sira's View of Women: A Literary Analysis* (Chico, CA: Scholars, 1982), 19ff., in Tucker and Liefeld, *Daughters of the Church*, 42.

Lie #1
God created women as inferior beings, destined to serve their husbands.

1. *Oerves de Galen*, ed. and trans. C. Daremberg (Paris: Bailliere, 1856) 2.99, quoted in Gerald C. Tiffin, "The Problem of Credulity in Women," in Carrol D. Osburn (Ed.), *Essays on Women in Earliest Christianity, Vol. 2* (Joplin, MO: College Press Publishing, 1995), 409.

2. Augustine, *Literal Commentary on Genesis*, IX.5, quoted in Tucker and Liefeld, *Daughters of the Church*, 123.

3. John Knox, *The First Blast of the Trumpet Against the Monstrous Regiment of Women*, (1558), quoted in Tucker and Liefeld, *Daughters of the Church*, 177.

4. Thomas Aquinas, *Summa Theologica* (Matriti: Biblioteca de Autores Cristianos, 1955), 1.680–85, quoted in Osburn, *Essays on Women in Earliest Christianity, Vol. 2*, 416.

5. M. Burrows, "Female Education," *Quarterly Review*, 126 (1869), 144–145, quoted in Osburn, *Essays on Women in Earliest Christianity, Vol. 2*, 431.

6. Phyllis Thompson, *A Transparent Woman: The Compelling Story of Gladys Aylward* (Grand Rapids, MI: Zondervan, 1971), 183, quoted in Tucker and Liefeld, *Daughters of the Church*, 327.

7. Helen Kooiman Kaiser, *Kathryn Kuhlman* (Old Tappan, NJ: Revell, 1971), 99, quoted in Tucker and Liefeld, *Daughters of the Church*, 393.

8. Earl Lavender, "Tertullian–Against Women?" in *On the Apparel of Women*, 1.1.1–2, quoted in Osburn, *Essays on*

Women in Earliest Christianity, Vol. 2, 332–333.

9. Martin Luther, quoted in Will Durant, *The Reformation: A History of European Civilization from Wycliffe to Calvin, 1300–1564* (New York: Simon and Shuster, 1957), 416, quoted in Tucker and Liefeld, *Daughters of the Church,* 173.

10. Gerald C. Tiffin, "The Problem of Credulity in Women," in Osburn, *Essays on Women in Earliest Christianity, Vol. 2,* 431. In Victorian England, women were denied access to university education because their culture told them that women were not as capable as men of learning. One writer, M. Burrows, said in 1869 that female minds were "ill prepared for hard and regular study."

11. Catherine Booth, *Female Ministry: Women's Right to Preach the Gospel* (London: Salvation Army Printing and Publishing Offices, 1859) 22.

12. Eve is called *ezer,* the Hebrew word for *help,* in Genesis 2:18. This is the same word that is used to describe God as divine Helper in Deuteronomy 33:7, 26, 29 and Psalms 33:20; 70:5; 115:9–11; 146:5. Because the same word is used to describe God, it cannot imply that Eve was inferior to Adam. We should also note that the term *helper* is used to describe the Holy Spirit in John 14–16.

Lie #2
Women are not equipped to assume leadership roles in the church.

1. John Chrysostom, *The Kind of Women Who Ought to Be Taken as Wives,* quoted in Elizabeth A. Clark, *Women in the Early Church* (Wilmington, DE: Michael Glazier, 1983), 37, in Tucker and Liefeld, *Daughters of the Church,* 124.

2. Francois de Salignac de la Mothe-Fenelon, *Education des Filles* (Paris: E. Flammarion, 1937 reprint), in Osburn (Ed.), *Essays on Women in Earliest Christianity, Vol. 2,* 427.

3. John Milton Williams, "Women's Suffrage," *Bsac 50* (April 1893), 343, in Osburn (ed.), *Essays on Women in Earliest Christianity, Vol. 2,* 461.

4. Source obtained from the Internet: John MacArthur, "Grace to You" ministry website. An answer to the

question, "Can women serve as elders in the church?"
www.gty.org/Curiosity_Shop/womenelders.

5. Osburn (ed.), *Essays on Women in Earliest Christianity,*
   Vol. 2, 460.
6. From a sermon by Billy Sunday, quoted in "The Fighting
   Saint," *The Trenton (N.J.) Evening Times*, Jan. 6, 1916, in
   Osburn (ed.), *Essays on Women in Earliest Christianity,*
   Vol. 2, 464.
7. Mark L. Pinsky, "Women Pastors May Lose Pulpit," *The
   Orlando Sentinel*, May 19, 2000, A1, 12.
8. Craig Keener, *The IVP Bible Background Commentary:
   New Testament* (Madison, WI: Intervarsity Press, 1993),
   447–448.
9. Dr. Kenneth E. Bailey, "Women Leaders," from the videotape series Women in the New Testament, (Wichita, KS:
   Harvest Communications, Inc.).
10. Ibid.
11. Booth, *Female Ministry*, 5.

Lie #3

Women must not teach or preach to men in a church setting.

1. Mishna Sotah 3.4; B. Sotah 20a. It should be noted that the
   Jewish Talmud is a collection of comments by rabbis who
   disagree, and the statement here about the "obscenity" of
   teaching women the law of God is challenged. However,
   many scholars of early Jewish thought believe the quote here
   represents the prevalent opinion of rabbis in the first century. Women were not allowed to study the Torah or to
   become disciples of rabbis.
2. Origen, *Fragments on I Corinthians*, quoted in Tucker and
   Liefeld, *Daughters of the Church,* 106.
3. Anonymous, "Have Women Immortal Souls? The Popular
   Belief Disputed" (London: Frederich Farah, n.d.), 5, in
   Osburn (ed.), *Essays on Women in Earliest Christianity,*
   Vol. 2, 483.
4. Jamie Buckingham, *Daughter of Destiny: Kathryn
   Kuhlman, Her Story* (Old Tappan, NJ: Fleming H. Revell,

1976), 125–6, in Tucker and Liefeld, *Daughters of the Church,* 392–3.

5. "Women in the Church: Scriptural Principles and Ecclesiastical Practice" in J. Gordon Melton (ed.), *The Churches Speak on Women's Ordination: Offical Statements from Religious Bodies and Ecumenical Organizations* (Detroit: Gale Research, Inc., 1991), 134, in Susan Hill Lindley, *You Have Stept Out of Your Place: A History of Women and Religion in America* (Louisville, KY: Westminister John Knox Press, 1996), 368.

6. David Van Biema, "The Preacher's Daughter," *Time,* May 1, 2000, 56–7.

7. Richard and Catherine Clark Kroeger, *I Suffer Not a Woman* (Grand Rapids, MI: Baker Book House, 1992), 87–98.

8. Although Richard and Catherine Clark Kroeger offer several possible meanings of the Greek verb *authentein,* which in 1 Timothy 2:12 is usually translated "to have authority over" or "to usurp authority from," they believe it could be translated "to declare oneself to be the author of." Because some gnostic priestesses believed woman was actually created before man, it is possible that they were teaching the church at Ephesus that woman was the originator of man—and therefore man's superior. This would explain why the apostle Paul stepped in to stop these particular women from having any influence on the young church. See Kroger, *I Suffer Not a Woman,* 103–4.

9. Walter C. Kaiser, Jr., "Shared Leadership," *Christianity Today,* October 3, 1986, 124; Joseph H. Thayer, *Thayer's Greek-English Lexicon of the New Testament* (Nashville, TN: Baker Book House Co., Broadman Press, 1977), 275.

10. Thayer, *Thayer's Greek-English Lexicon of the New Testament,* 17.

11. Kenneth S. Kantzer, "Proceed With Care," *Christianity Today,* October 3, 1986.

Lie #4
A woman should view her husband as the "priest of the home."

1. Thomas Aquinas, quoted in Will Durant, *The Age of Faith* (New York: simon and Shuster, 1950), 826, in Tucker and Liefeld, *Daughters of the Church,* 164.
2. John R. Rice, *Bobbed Hair, Bossy Wives and Women Preachers: Significant Questions for Honest Christian Women Settled by the Word of God* (Wheaton, IL: Sword of the Lord Publishers, 1941) 15, in Susan Hill Lindley, *You Have Stept Out of Your Place: A History of Women and Religion in America,* 347.
3. Letha Scanzoni, quoted in Tucker and Liefeld, *Daughters of the Church,* 411.
4. Ibid., 76.
5. Ibid.
6. Ibid., 54.
7. Rebecca Merrill Groothuis, *Good News for Women* (Grand Rapids, MI: Baker Books, 1997), 156–7.
8. Eusebius, *Ecclesiastical History*, in Tucker and Liefeld, *Daughters of the Church,* 113.
9. Ibid., 114.
10. Ibid.
11. For more detailed information about female martyrs in church history, see *Foxe's Book of Martyrs* (Grand Rapids, MI: Fleming H Revell, 1999).
12. Tucker and Liefeld, *Daughters of the Church,* 214–5.

Lie #5
A man needs to "cover" a woman in her ministry activities.

1. Argula von Grumback, quoted in Roland H. Bainton, *Women of the Reformation in Germany and Italy* (Austin, TX: Augsburg, n.d.), 105, in Tucker and Liefeld, *Daughters of the Church,* 185.
2. Richard Mather, *Church Government and Church Covenant Discussed,* (London: 1643), 60, in Tucker and Liefeld, *Daughters of the Church,* 220.
3. Quoted in Frances Willard, *Woman in the Pulpit*, in Tucker

and Liefeld, *Daughters of the Church,* 220.

4. These concepts appear in the manual for Bill Gothard's Institute in Basic Youth Conflicts seminar, 1969. See section entitled, "Principles of God's Chain of Command."

5. Katherine Bushnell, *God's Word to Women,* 110–113.

6. Judy Brown, *Women Ministers According to Scripture,* (Kearney, NE: Morris Publishing, 1996), 250.

7. Kantzer, "Proceed With Care."

Lie #6
Women who exhibit strong leadership qualities pose a serious danger to the church.

1. Jane Hunter, *The Gospel of Gentility: American Women Missionaries in Turn-of-the-Century China* (New Haven, Connecticut: Yale University Press, 1984), 13–14, in Tucker and Liefeld, *Daughters of the Church,* 302.

2. Fred Smith, quoted in Gaile Bederman, "'The Women Have Had Charge of the Church Work Long Enough': The Men and Religion Forward Movement of 1911–1912 and the Masculinization of Middle Class Protestantism." *American Quarterly* 41, 1989, in Osburn (Ed.), *Essays on Women in Earliest Christianity,* Vol. 2, 464.

3. Source obtained from the Internet: David Cloud, "Women Preachers," Fundamentalist Baptist Information Service, Jan. 30, 1998. www.whidbey.net/~dcloud/fbns/womenpreachers.

4. Jane Wilson James, *Women in American Religion* (Philadelphia: University of Pennsylvania Press, 1980), 20, in Tucker and Liefeld, *Daughters of the Church,* 387.

5. For biographies of these pioneer missionaries, see Lewis and Betty Drummond, *Women of Awakenings: The Historic Contribution of Women to Revival Movements* (Grand Rapids, MI: Kregel Publications, 1997).

6. Susan Lill Lindley, *You Have Stept Out of Your Place,* 336–7.

7. "Ministering Women: A forum with Jill Briscoe, Mary Kassian, Jean Thompson, and Miriam Adeney," moderated

by Wendy Murray Zoba and Helen Lee, *Christianity Today,*
April 8, 1996, 14.

8. Tucker and Liefeld, *Daughters of the Church,* 177.

Lie #7
Women are more easily deceived than men.

1. Tertullian, On the Apparel of Women, 1.1, quoted in
   Osburn (ed.), *Essays on Women in Earliest Christianity,*
   Vol. 2, 411.
2. Salimbene, quoted in G.G. Coulton, *From St. Francis to
   Dante: A Translation of All that Is of Primary Interest in the
   Chronicle of the Franciscan Salimbene,* (London: D. Nutt,
   1906), 91–92, in Osburn (ed.), *Essays on Women in Earliest
   Christianity, Vol. 2,* 419.
3. Heinrich Kramer and James Sprenger, *Malleus Maleficarum
   (The Witch's Hammer)* (New York: Dover, 1971), 41–44, in
   Osburn (ed.), *Essays on Women in Earliest Christianity,*
   Vol. 2, 425–6.
4. Susan Hill Lindley, *You have Stept Out of Your Place,* 3–7.
5. Tucker and Liefeld, *Daughters of the Church,* 220–4.
6. Ibid., 222.
7. Andy Butcher, "The Truth About the Salem Witch Trials,"
   Charisma, October 1999, 50–1.
8. Source obtained from the Internet: David Cloud,
   "Women Preachers," Fundamentalist Baptist
   Information Service, Jan. 30, 1998.
   www.whidbey.net/~dcloud/fbns/womenpreachers.
9. Tucker and Liefeld, *Daughters of the Church,* 61. Tucker
   and Liefeld point out that this prayer of thanksgiving for
   being male appeared in most early Jewish traditions,
   including the Babylonian Talmud, the Tosephta and the
   Jerusalem Talmud.
10. From the Talmud, B. Pesahim 62b, quoted in Tucker and
    Liefeld, *Daughters of the Church,* 61.
11. Kroeger, *I Suffer Not a Woman,* 143–4.
12. Osburn (Ed.), *Essays on Women in Earliest Christianity,*
    Vol. 2, 417.

13. Tucker and Liefeld, *Daughters of the Church,* 166.
14. Source obtained from the Internet: Helen Ellerbe, *The Dark Side of Christian History* (San Rafael, CA: Morningstar Books, 1995), Chapter 8. www.warmcove.com/morningstar/chapter8.
15. Ibid.
16. There is considerable dispute today over how many women actually died in Europe during the Medieval Witch Hunt period. At one time some historians speculated that the number of women executed could have been as high as nine million. During the 1970s, Americans involved in Wicca and other neo-pagan religions began to study the subject extensively, and some were guilty of exaggerating the accounts or of using spurious information. But today, even practitioners of Wicca are rethinking the issue. Medieval historian Jenny Gibbons, who is a professing neo-pagan, says less than fifteen thousand confirmed executions for witchcraft have been discovered in all of Europe and North America. Brian Levack, author of *The Witch Hunt in Early Modern Europe,* calculates that there were approximately one hundred ten thousand witch trials during the period, but he suggests that only 48 percent of the trials ended in execution. That would put the total death count near sixth thousand people. Gibbons and others also point out that not all the accused were women. She proposes that in most cases about 75 percent to 80 percent were women, but in some countries, including Iceland, a majority of the accused were men.
17. See Allan Kardec, *Spirits' Book* (Kila, MT: Kessinger Publishing, reprinted from 1898).
18. Walter Martin, *The Kingdom of the Cults* (Minneapolis: Bethany House Publishers, 1965), 187–9.
19. Source obtained from the Internet: "Introduction to Crowley Studies," www.maroney.org/CrowleyIntro/Christianity.
20. See Gerald Gardner, Gardner Witchcraft Series (Hendersonville, NC: Mercury Publishing, 1999).

21. Source obtained from the Internet: "About Edgar Cayce," Association for Research and Enlightenment, www.are-cayce.com.
22. Martin, *The Kingdom of the Cults*, 345–350.
23. Ibid., 126–129. Martin points out that Mary Baker Eddy actually plagiarized manuscripts of Dr. P.P. Quimby to write her book, *Science and Health with Key to the Scriptures*.
24. Richard and Catherine Clark Kroeger, *I Suffer Not a Woman*, 161–170.

Lie #8
Women can't be fulfilled or spiritually effective without a husband and children.

1. John Chrysostom, *Homilies on Timothy*, in Gerald C. Tiffin, "The Problem of Credulity in Women," quoted in Osburn, *Essays on Women in Earliest Christianity, Vol. 2*, 413.
2. Vern Bullough, "Medieval Medical and Scientific Views of Women," Viator 4 (1973), 499 in Osburn (ed.), *Essays on Women in Earliest Christianity, Vol. 2*, 414.
3. Martin Luther, quoted in Gerald C. Tiffin, "The Problem of Credulity in Women," quoted in Osburn, *Essays on Women in Earliest Christianity, Vol. 2*, 423.
4. Teresa of Avila, in Hannah Ward and Jennifer Wild (eds.), *The Doubleday Christian Quotation Collection* (New York: Doubleday, 1997), 104.
5. Source obtained from the Internet: Mary Ann Jeffreys, "Macrina: Monastic Pioneer," women.crosswalk.com/columns/history.
6. Source obtained from the Internet: Mary Ann Jeffreys, "Hildegarde: A Light in the Dark Ages," women.crosswalk.com/columns/history.
7. Source obtained from the Internet: Mary Ann Jeffreys, "Catherine of Siena: Radical Lover of God," women.crosswalk.com/columns/history.
8. Source obtained from the Internet: Mary Ann Jeffreys, "Holy Hannah and Her Circle of Friends," women.crosswalk.com/columns/history.
9. "Lottie Moon," Southern Baptist Historical Library and Archives, 1998.

10. Janet and George Benge, *Mary Slessor* (Seattle: YWAM Publishing, 1999) 141–150.

11. Source obtained from the Internet:
    Mary Ann Jeffreys, "Henrietta Mears: Coach of a Dream Team," women.crosswalk.com/columns/history.

12. Source obtained from the Internet: Jessica Longaker, "The Role of Women in Mormonism," 1995, exmormon.org. For further information on the false teachings of Mormonism, see Walter Martin, *The Kingdom of the Cults* (Minneapolis, MN: Bethany House Publishers, 1965) 166–226.

13. Anne Dickason, "Anatomy and Destiny: The Role of Biology in Plato's Views of Women," in Carol C. Gould and Marx W. Wartofsky (eds.), *Women and Philosophy: Toward a Theory of Liberation* (New York: Putnam, 1976).

14. Caroline Whitbeck, "Theories of Sex Difference," in Gould and Marx W. Wartofsky (eds.), *Women and Philosophy: Toward a Theory of Liberation* (New York: n.p., 1976).

15. Kroeger, *I Suffer Not a Woman,* 176–177.

16. Katherine Bushnell, *God's Word to Women,* 160.

Lie #9
Women shouldn't work outside the home.

1. Martin Luther, quoted in Julia O'Faolain and Lauro Martines (eds.), *Not in God's Image* (New York: Harper and Row, 1973) 180, in Tucker and Liefeld, *Daughters of the Church,* 173.

2. Menno Simons, *The True Christian Faith*, from John C. Wenger, ed., *The Complete Writings of Menno Simons,* (Scottsdale, PA: Herald, 1956), 376–83, quoted in Tucker and Liefeld, *Daughters of the Church,* 178.

3. From *The Lutheran Witness,* quoted in Janet James, *Women in American Religion* (Philadelphia: University of Pennsylvania, 1980), 231, in Tucker and Liefeld, *Daughters of the Church,* 284.

4. Paisley Dodds, "Church Closes Day Care to Get Moms Home," *The Seattle Times,* April 4, 1997.

5. Mary A. Quigley and Loretta Kaufman, *And What Do You Do?: When Women Choose to Stay at Home* (Berkeley, CA: Wildcat Canyon Press, 2000).

6. Rebecca Merrill Groothuis, *Women Caught in the Conflict: The Culture War Between Traditionalism and Feminism* (Eugene, OR: WIPF & Stock Publishers, 1994) 3.

7. Ibid., 4.

8. Ronald Fletcher, *The Family and Marriage in Britain* (New York: Pelican, 1980), 13, quoted in Osburn, *Essays on Women in Earliest Christianity, Vol. 2*, 435. Fletcher points out that women in Victorian England were expected to remain in the home in order to protect them from the outside world. The idea that woman are delicate and inferior "allowed the husband the right to seek sexual pleasure elsewhere," Fletcher writes. This view "disabled women psychologically and physically. It also disabled them legally, for outside the home, women suffered the same legal status as lunatics and children."

9. Source obtained from the Internet: Lucretia Mott, "Discource on Women," December 17, 1849. Gifts of Speech, gos.sbc.edu/mott.

10. For further reading on Harriett Beecher Stowe, see Forrest Wilson, *Crusader in Crinoline: The Life of Harriet Beecher Stowe* (Philadelphia: Lippincott, 1941).

11. For further reading on Jane Addams, see Allen F. Davis, *American Heroine: The Life and Legend of Jane Addams* (New York: Oxford University Press, 1973).

12. For further reading on Clara Barton, see David H. Burton, *Clara Barton: In the Service of Humanity* (Westport, CT: Greenwood Press).

13. Source obtained from the Internet: "Alice Evans," National Women's Hall of Fame. www.greatwomen.org/evans.

14. For further reading on Rachael Carson, see Terry Tempest Williams, "The Spirit of Rachel Carson," *Audubon Magazine*, July–August 1992.

15. For more information on women's achievements in medicine and science, go to the National Women's Hall of Fame at www.greatwomen.org/evans.

16. To see a copy of the first page of Virginia Apgar's

proposal on the health of infants written in 1953, go to www.apgarfamily.com/virginia.

Lie #10
Women must obediently submit to their husbands in all situations.

1. Friar Cherubino, quoted in Grant L. Martin, *Counseling for Family Violence and Abuse*, 23.
2. Martin Luther, quoted in Tucker and Liefield, *Daughters of the Church*, 174.
3. Susan Brooks Thistlethwaite, quoted in Phyllis and James M. Alsdurf, "Wife Abuse and Scripture," in Anne L. Horton and Judith A. Williamson (eds.), *Abuse and Religion: When Praying Isn't Enough*, (Lexington, MA: Lexington Books, 1988), 222.
4. Marcia Ford, "The Silent Shame," *Charisma*, March 1995, 46.
5. James M. and Phyllis Alsdurf, "A Pastoral Response," in Horton and Williamson (eds.), *Abuse and Religion*, 165–18.
6. Ibid., 225–226.
7. Catherine Clark Kroeger, "The Classical Concept of 'Head' as 'Source,'" (Appendix III) in Gretchen Gaebelein Hull, *Equal to Serve* (Grand Rapids, MI: Baker Books), 279–281.
8. "Blood and Honor," *Middle East Intelligence Digest*, February 1995, 4.
9. "Honor Crimes: Facts From Amnesty International/UNICEF," The Associated Press, *The Orlando Sentinel*, July 2, 2000, A–15.
10. "Family Pride Drives Even Mothers to Kill," The Associated Press, *The Orlando Sentinel*, July 2, 2000, A–15.
11. *Time*, January 9, 1995, quoted in *Middle East Intelligence Digest*, February 1995, 5.
12. Elisabeth Farrell, "What the Qur'an Says About Women," *Charisma*, June 2000, 90–91.
13. Source obtained from the Internet: "Women in Hinduism," geocities.com/~abdulwahid/muslimarticles/ hindu_women.
14. A complete timeline of the women's suffrage movement is available womenshistory.about.com/homework/ womenshistory/library/weekly/aa031600a.

15. Martin, *Counseling for Family Violence and Abuse*, 23.
16. Ibid., 24.
17. Ford, "The Silent Shame," 45.

Conclusion

1. George Fox, *The Works of George Fox* (New York: Isaac T. Hopper, 1831), reprint ed. New York: AMS, 1975), vol. 4:106,9, in Tucker and Liefeld, *Daughters of the Church*, 227.
2. Catherine Booth, *Female Ministry*, in Tucker and Liefeld, *Daughters of the Church*, 264.
3. Katherine Bushnell, *God's Word to Women*, 324.
4. Jerena Lee, *Religious Experiences and Journal* (Philadelphia: Jerena Lee, 1849), in Tucker and Liefeld, *Daughters of the Church*, 259–60.
5. Source obtained from the Internet: David Yonggi Cho, "Don't Be Afraid to Empower Women." From the transcript of a sermon preached in February 1999 at the Crowns of Beauty Conference in Italy, www.dawnministries.org/reports/report_41.
6. Source obtained from the Internet: Sheryl Wingerd, "Women Are God's Secret Weapon," www.dawnministries.org/reports/report_41.
7 From a telephone interview with "Brother Michael," missionary to China. July 14, 2000.
8. Lottie Moon, quoted in Tucker and Liefeld, *Daughters of the Church*, 303.
9. "Solemn Assembly of the International Pentecostal Holiness Church" (Oklahoma City, OK: IPHC Resource Center, August 23–4, 1996), not copyrighted.
10. William Booth, quoted in Flora Larson, *My Best Men Are Women* (London: Hodder and Stoughton, 1974), 22, in Tucker and Liefeld, *Daughters of the Church*, 266.
11. Gretchen Gaebelein Hull, *Equal to Serve*, 56.
12. Billy Bruce, "Jesus and the Hot Mamas," *Charisma*, August 1999, 52.
13. Hope Flinchbaugh, "Floods of Love in Mozambique," *Charisma*, June 2000, 73–84.